HOW TO GET THE BEST
OUT OF TODAY'S SALESPEOPLE

Also by the same author:

101 Ways to Boost Your Performance
Close Close Close
How to Double Your Profits Within the Year
How to Sell Your Higher Price
How to Win New Customers
Selling – the Most Important Job in the World

*For a complete list of Management Books 2000 titles
visit our website on http://www.mb2000.com*

HOW TO GET THE BEST
OUT OF TODAY'S SALESPEOPLE

John Fenton

2000

First published in Great Britain in 1999 by Management Books 2000 Ltd,
Cowcombe House,
Cowcombe Hill,
Chalford,
Gloucestershire GL6 8HP
Tel: 01285-760722. Fax: 01285-760708
e-mail: MB2000@compuserve.com
web-site: www.mb2000.com

Printed and bound in Great Britain by Biddles, Guildford

British Library Cataloguing in Publication Data is available

ISBN 1-85252-282-8

Contents

Acknowledgements

The writing of this book has been something of a combined effort.

Thanks are due to the countless number of sales managers and sales directors who have let me train them and their sales forces – so many that they have to be nameless – for the many proven more successful techniques for getting the best out of today's salespeople which they allowed me to include in this book.

Special thanks go to another author, John Harman, whose four business novels, Money for Nothing, The Bottom Line, Called to Account and Dangerous Assets have given me much stimulation and whose word processor has generated the final copy for this edition.

John and I go back twenty years to when we wrote sales training films together, so when I needed help to beat my copy deadline, his was the number I rang.

VISION STATEMENT

The Profession of Selling

It is a glaring glimpse of the obvious to say that no amount of production is of the slightest value unless the products are sold for cash.

Selling is the very crux of any commercial or industrial enterprise.

It therefore stands to reason that, as a nation which depend so heavily on selling our products abroad, it is very much in the national interest that the highest standards and the most advanced techniques in salesmanship should be encouraged.

HRH Prince Philip

Duke of Edinburgh KG, KT

A

Abilities

Okay, so you've made it!

You're either a newly-appointed sales manager – the 'new kid on the block', eager to learn the job and succeed in getting the best out of your sales people – or you're an experienced sales manager, an old hand, but one who's still enthusiastic about improving your own and your sales force's performance.

Whichever you are, your success starts with **attitude**. And, for the rest of your successful sales management career, it continues with attitude.

The *right* attitude.

By reading this book, you are giving evidence of the right attitude and revealing a commitment – a commitment to discovering the methods and principles of sales management that bring success. You are showing a resolve to learn techniques which have *proven* to be successful. Techniques I've been teaching for years and which have brought me success.

The right attitude means working hard to hone your skills, being prepared to discover all you can and learning everything vital to the job. And one of the first things to learn is that your new job as a sales manager is not your old job as a salesperson writ large.

Many sales managers remain, primarily, super salespeople – still 'one of the gang'. This affects their relationship with their salespeople, particularly in the crucial tasks of development and supervision of subordinates.

Sometimes, this desire to remain one of the gang emanates from the fact that the newly appointed sales manager was not the top salesperson in the company. He or she is conscious of this and feels almost guilty, which drives the newcomer to be accepted, to perform every task within the new area of responsibility as well as he or she always did – and better than anyone else.

Crazy! It's like a chicken farmer believing he should be the one who lays the eggs.

A sales manager doesn't have to be a better salesperson than his or her salespeople. Although there are always exceptions, the best salespeople seldom make the best sales managers.

And that's your goal. To be the best sales manager.

How?

Think back to your time as a salesperson.

You probably had a natural **aptitude** (*a propensity or talent*) for Selling. However, that wasn't enough. You needed **application** (*sustained or concentrated effort*) to develop those aptitudes. You went on sales training courses (mine, hopefully) and did a lot or reading and self-development work. Which gave you the **ability** (*capacity or power*) to do the job well.

Then, someone in authority in your organisation recognised your abilities. They saw you had some of the **attributes** (*characteristic qualities*) that would make a good sales manager.

So here you are – starting all over again.

However, the aptitudes and attributes that made you a good salesperson won't, by themselves, make you a good sales manager. You need to develop *new and different abilities* in the self-same way that you developed abilities as a salesperson – through **application**.

Reading this book is a good first step.

As a salesperson, your primary working relationship was with your customers. Now, as a sales manager, it's with your sales force.

To develop your abilities, you need to establish a new set of working relationships.

To help you bridge the gap between selling and managing, here's a comparison between the essential attributes of a good salesperson and the necessary abilities of a good sales manager:

ESSENTIAL ATTRIBUTES OF A GOOD SALESPERSON	NECESSARY ABILITIES OF A GOOD SALES MANAGER
Personal Drive (Ego Drive)	Submission of personal needs to the goals of the company (Corporate Drive)
Needs to win battles (on every call)	Needs to win the war (meet the Corporate Goals)
Able to work alone	Able to work with others
Gets customers to see his/her point	Gets sales team to see Company's point
Needs selling skills and product knowledge	Needs management skills and marketing knowledge
Able to work away from the office	Able to work at the office AND away from the office
Works well with people and numbers	Works well with people, figures, paperwork and the corporate hierarchy
Good at implementing sales tactics	Good at developing sales tactics and marketing strategy.
Gregarious. Likes to be with people but spends most of his/her time alone	Spends much of his/her time in the office with people. Would love time alone (uninterrupted) to be able to do the job.

Advertising

The point of the kind of advertising we are discussing here is to produce leads. It is a major part of the marketing mix. When companies are able to produce sales through advertising alone, they do it. There's no sales force. But most companies need a sales force. Thus, your job is to produce as many – and good – leads as your ad budget will allow.

But, if you have a sales force, why bother with advertising? A survey, conducted a few years ago, of about 1,100 British companies shows why.

Size of Company	Average number of persons who influence buying decisions	Average number of persons visited by salespeople
Less than 200 employees	3.43	1.72
200 to 400 employees	4.85	1.75
401 to 1,000 employees	5.81	1.90
More than 1,000 employees	6.50	1.65

How else can you get to all those decision influencers whom your salespeople are missing? And what about all those potential customers you didn't know existed?

A sales force, working in conjunction with advertising, can produce more sales than either one working alone. It's called synergy.

But, if sales are to work effectively with advertising, it is absolutely vital that the sales manager has a major influence on all creative aspects of the advertising campaign. Otherwise, it's possible for the sales force to be presented with an advertising campaign created by a slick advertising agency, as a *fait accompli* – a campaign which promotes a product or service they scarcely recognise to a market which bears no relation to reality.

The sales manager should be the first point of reference and the final arbiter in any advertising campaign. No one knows customers better than you. No one knows the benefits of the product and how customers employ those benefits, better than you. An agency or in-house advertising department can frequently have a distorted view or profile of customers and product benefits. Educate them.

Most clever, creative people in ad agencies or marketing departments can produce marvellous pictures and write succinct, punchy copy. (Why not? That's what they're paid for.) But only a sales manager can say whether the ad will actually work and produce sales or sales leads.

Designing Advertisements and Mail Shots that Pull more Inquiries

Always follow the AIDA format

ATTENTION	(Picture or simple headline)
INTEREST	(Carrot – preferably about money)
DESIRE	(What could be in it for the reader)
ACTION	(Fill in a coupon or pick up the phone)

Everyone in Advertising will tell you that a *right hand* page position is more effective than a left hand position, but do they ever tell you why? Here's the reason:

80% of people are *browsers* and l*eft-handed thumb flickers* – i.e. they hold the magazine in their right palm and flick through it from back to front with their left thumb.

The 1.5 Second Rule

This 80% of the world give you a maximum of 1.5 seconds (while they're flicking through) to get their attention. *Fail* to catch their attention – and you've lost them for ever.

How this applies to loose insert advertising – 80% of people shake loose inserts out of their magazine, straight into the waste bin. Your 1.5 seconds is the time it takes the loose insert to drop from the magazine into the bin. Objective: to make the shaker reach down and retrieve the loose insert from the bin.

A note or two on lettering

Upper and lower characters are clearer to read than capitals – and take up a lot less space, type size for type size. Clarity is a crucial key for gaining attention. Check the following example:

ISN'T IT THE FOOLISH MAN WHO KNOWS THE PRICE OF EVERYTHING AND THE VALUE OF NOTHING?

Isn't it the foolish man who knows the price of everything and the value of nothing?

Beware words reversed out of black. To most people, they are less clear than black type on white paper. Test: see how long it takes before you go 'ughh!'...

This is what happens when a fly
lands on your food.
Flies cannot eat solid food,
so to soften it up, they vomit on it.
Then they stamp the vomit in until
it's a liquid, usually stamping in a few germs
for good measure.
Then, when it's good and runny,
they suck it all back again,
probably dropping some excrement
at the same time.
And then, when they've finished eating,
it's your turn.

This is what happens when a fly
lands on your food.
Flies cannot eat solid food,
so to soften it up, they vomit on it.
Then they stamp the vomit in until
it's a liquid, usually stamping in a few germs
for good measure.
Then, when it's good and runny,
they suck it all back again,
probably dropping some excrement
at the same time.
And then, when they've finished eating,
it's your turn.

White space sells. Don't fill in the corners with words. Identity is also important. O rings are round, not square.

For quality impression, a type font with serifs, rather than a plain 'sans' face, will improve quality.

This example is sans:

This example is serif:

Pictures

- Always use a picture when you can.

- Use pictures with life in them.

- Avoid 'still life' pics of the product.

- If the product shot is a static piece of equipment or machinery, have people in the picture.

- Ask yourself, does the picture tell the main story?

Copy – Ask yourself the following:

- Does your copy create the desire?

- Does it tell the truth – and tell it well? No puffs?

- Does it talk about customers' successes with your product or service?

- Do you know what you wanted to say?

- Does your headline have a big promise?

- Is the Ad written in a pithy way?

- Is it easy to understand?

- Have you used short, Anglo-Saxon words?

- Do the words relate to the picture?

- Have you included the name of the product?

- Is your promise in any way 'unique'?

- If your spouse/partner read it, would he/she believe it?

- Have you created a 'telegram'?

- Remember, if you can feature customers in your advertising, you'll keep those customers for life.

Action

- Get the advert reader doing something.

- Responding to the advertisement works best with the use of coupons.

- If you use a coupon make sure it's on the outside edge or across the bottom of the page – this makes for a single cut.

- Don't put coupons on a cover page (people won't disfigure covers).

- Make sure the company name, address, phone, fax and other numbers are not only on the coupon – but are still on the ad after the coupon has been cut.

There are seven response methods you can use in an ad for the ACTION part:

1. Telephone a named individual
2. Fax a named individual
3. Write to a named individual
4. Call in on a named individual
5. E-mail a named individual
6. Fill in and return the coupon
7. Circle the relevant number on the reader-enquiry service card

Use as many of the seven as you can. Make it EASY for the customer to take ACTION.

Where to Advertise

The five main advertising media with their approximate ad spends are:

Newspapers, consumer magazines, trade, technical and professional publications	65.0%
Commercial television	28.0%
Hoardings, posters, transport, etc.	4%
Commercial radio	2.6%
Cinema	1.0%

Most ad campaigns supporting the sales force work best in print media.

The sales manager should also be consulted about which media are best to reach customers and potential customers (the target audience).

British Rate and Data (BRAD) – published monthly by Maclean Hunter Ltd, London – lists all UK print media. Most of the journals listed have 'readership profiles' supplied by the publishers. However, both you and your sales people already know which journals and magazines your customers read. You see them in their offices. And you know where your competitors advertise. But always keep your eyes open for any new journals being read by your customers.

The UK Audit Bureau of Circulations (ABC) produces circulation figures for print media. These are published in BRAD. Check which journals give the most punch for your pound. But look also at readership breakdown. The selected journal may have a 20,000 ABC circulation, but perhaps only 25% of that circulation goes to your particular customers. This means that the cost of advertising in that journal will cost you *four times* the cost per thousand as shown in BRAD.

Ad Placement

If you advertise in trade directories, reference books and other publications with a long life, try to get an ad on the Bookmark or facing the contents page. Ads on the spine also work well.

In trade and technical journals, try to obtain the page facing the numbers side of the journal's reader enquiry cards.

Also, try to get your advert close to or facing that editorial page in the journal featuring the 'gossip'. Everybody, no matter what their business, likes to read light-hearted pieces about who's doing what, who's been promoted, who's been embarrassed and so on. Ads close to those editorial pieces will have a higher 'traffic' than elsewhere.

Remember the KISS principle works as well in advertising as in any other part of the business:

Keep It Simple, Stupid.

When you get a response from An Advert or Mail Shot,

DON'T POST LITERATURE

If you do, you'll reduce your salespeople's chance of winning the appointment by at least 70%.

And you won't even find out why the respondent took the trouble to respond.

DATE POSTED	NCR 3: white pink blue	LFU NUMBER
TERRITORY NUMBER	**LEAD FOLLOW UP**	

ENQUIRER	NAME	JOB TITLE

COMPANY ADDRESS AND POSTCODE

TELEPHONE NUMBER

ADVERTISEMENT

PUBLICATION		DATE OF ISSUE

LEAD FOLLOW-UP

1. Identify that you are speaking to the right person.
   IS THAT MR .... ?

2. Tell him who you are. Use your first name and surname.
   'GOOD MORNING, MY NAME IS .... OF ....(company)

3. Set the scene for him to tell you WHY he enquired.
   'THANK YOU FOR SENDING IN THE COUPON FROM
   OUR ADVERTISEMENT FOR .... IN .... I HAVE A
   LOT OF INFORMATION I CAN SEND YOU, BUT JUST
   TO MAKE SURE THAT I SEND YOU EXACTLY WHAT
   YOU WANT, WHAT MADE YO

4. Shut up and write down what he says

5. Ask a few questions relevant to 4 to help you decide
   whether to make an appointment or post him the
   MINIMUM literature. As soon as you have decided,
   STOP asking questions.
   SAMPLE QUESTIONS
   'Where do you buy from at present?
   'What are you paying at present?
   'How often do you use these?
   'How long has this been a problem?
   'Who else are you talking to?
   DO NOT GET INVOLVED in a technical discussion

6. If you decide to go for an appointment, finish like this:
   'WELL, I CERTAINLY THINK WE CAN HELP YOU.
   LOOK, I'VE GOT SOME DATA ON WHAT WE HAVE
   DONE FOR OTHER BUSINESSES THAT I'D LIKE TO
   SHOW YOU. I'M IN YOUR AREA (consult diary) NEXT
   .... CAN YOU SPARE ME TEN MINUTES, SAY, AT
   .... OR WOULD .... BE MORE CONVENIENT?

7. If you decide to send him the MINIMUM literature, tell him
   what it will be and staple your business card to the top
   and post it yourself TODAY.

**DON'T follow up a
lead with a letter and
literature**

**ALWAYS follow up
FAST with a
telephone call**

**And don't play it off
the seat of your pants
.... always use a
WORD TRACK**

**Anything less is
criminal negligence**

PINK COPY DUE BACK
TO HQ NO LATER THAN

Ambition

Ambition is a good thing. It's what your career is all about. It's what the profession of Selling is all about. But make sure your ambitions are legitimate and realistic.

Wanting to conquer the world is not a good ambition. (Nobody has done it yet.) Wanting to *save* the world is a good ambition – but probably impossible. (Nobody has done it yet.)

Wanting to be a multi-millionaire before you're thirty-five is laudable, but not if it means destroying yourself, wrecking your family and giving up all semblance of a normal life. Remember that nobody on their death bed ever said, 'I wish I'd spent more time at work.'

Work out your ambitions. Make sure they're legitimate and ethical – then go for them.

Right now, your only ambition is getting the best out of your sales people.

Analysing Your Customer Base

Size of Company by Annual Purchase	% of total customers	% of Total Sales	% of Total Calls	% of Total Profit	Average Order Value	Customer Category
More than £25K	6%	28%	11%	38%	More than £2K	A
£10K to £25K	16%	48%	17%	52%	£201 - £2K	B
£2K to £10K	30%	14%	38%	8%	£50 - £200	C
Less than £2K	40%	10%	34%	2%	Less than £50	D

1. 22% of customers (A + B) generated 76% of sales.
    78% of customers (C + D) generated 24% of sales.

2. 76% of sales (A + B) only received 28% of selling time.
    The remaining 24% of sales (C + D) received 72% of selling time.

3. 22% of customers (A + B) produced 90% of the profit (Gross Margin) but only received 28% of selling time.
    The remaining 78% of customers (C + D) took up 72% of selling time while only producing 10% of the total profit.

4. 48% of customers (D) received 34% of selling time while contributing only 2% profit with AOVs of less than £50.

What changes would you make to ensure an increase in both effective activity and results for the forthcoming year? What can you do to improve sales and profit – *and time allocations*?

One of the first things you need to do as a Sales Manager is to analyse your existing customer base. It will probably take you three months – not of solid work, because you will be getting data from various sources, but the task is well worth while, because the analysis will show you where your sales force is spending its time and tell you clearly what re-directing is urgently necessary.

The above is an example of a complete analysis for a company that, at the time it was done, was only selling by sales force – they had no tele-selling.

You shouldn't find it hard to improve results.

B

Bringing In Your Best Bets

How to take stock of the business in the pipeline

For *every* single piece of business, and independently of everything else, **QUESTION IT** (manager and salesperson together).

> Would *you* buy it, if you were the customer? Why would you?

If in doubt, check back on how you sold it:

> Which opening carrots would have aroused *your* interest?

> Did you use them?

> Which benefits would *you* have considered worthwhile?

> Did you stress them?

> What objections would *you* have raised? Did the customer?

> If he didn't, might he have been thinking about asking?

BE HONEST – then take a fresh look at that live quotation you submitted following your sales presentation...

WOULD YOU LIKE TO DO IT AGAIN – BUT BETTER?
SO WHAT'S STOPPING YOU?

There's no rule that says you can't. The customer is bound to be impressed by your concern. This is a top priority task to be conducted during the once every month 'On-the-Job Appraisal Day'. It should be a personal discussion between manager and salesperson.

Next Month's Best Bets – Making sure they happen

This checklist can be used in conjunction with the monthly BEST BETS LIST (see opposite).

Orders secured during the next two to three months will mainly come from the quotations that have already been submitted.

You need to find out:

1. Does the quotation meet requirements?

2. Are there any doubts or queries?

3. If yes ...   can we take the customer to see one working in another company?

4. If no ...   has the budget been approved?

5. If yes ...   can we have the order?

6. If no ...   when will the budget be approved?
   what can we do to help?
   is there anyone else who isn't completely satisfied that this is a good investment for the customer company?

7. Is the customer considering any other suppliers?

8. If yes ...   what are we up against?

9. Which supplier does the customer prefer?

10. Why?

11. Can we put together a comparison list of the advantages of each one?

12. If that clears up any doubts the customer had, can we go ahead?

Note: The Sales Manager should be looking for progression. No outstanding quotation must be allowed to remain static for longer than two months, unless there is a *very* good reason.

| BEST BETS LIST | | FOR MONTH..................... | | | SALESPERSON............................ | | | | | | |

FORECAST
THIS MONTH ---------------- £ _____
NEXT MONTH ---------------- £ _____
FOLLOWING MONTH ----- £ _____

ACTUAL ACHIEVED
THIS MONTH ---- £ _____ %
DEVIATION
FROM FORECAST _____%

		CUSTOMER	PRODUCTS	ORDER VALUE	BUDGET AOPPROVED	PROPOSAL APPROVED	FINANCIAL JUSTIFICATION	DEMONSTRATION OKAY	BOARD APPROVED	ORDER DATE	COMPETITION	POSSIBLE DELAYS AND NEXT ACTION
CUSTOMERS WHO WILL DEFINITELY ORDER NEXT MONTH	1											
	2											
	3											
	4											
	5											
	6											
PROBABLES BUT NOT YET DEFINITES												

Budgets

Budgets are about control. As the business of business is profit – revenue minus costs – it is obvious that not only must you forecast what sales you will produce in the next accounting period (usually a year), but also what the cost of getting those sales will be.

Sales department costs are mainly fixed: salaries, cost of cars, telephone, etc. There are a few variable costs, perhaps bonuses and incentive schemes, though these are not really very variable.

Budgeting not only forces you to think through what you're going to spend for the year, it also forces you to pinpoint your **break-even** – the sales level at which you move from loss to profitability.

Break-even is worked out as follows:

$$B/E = \frac{F \times S}{S - V}$$

where B/E = break even point, F = fixed costs,
S = selling price per unit, and V = variable costs per unit

For example, if values are as follows:

$$F = £50,000 \quad S = £10 \quad V = £2$$

Then,
$$B/E = \frac{£50,000 \times 10}{10 - 2}$$

In other words, break-even is £62,500 or 6,250 units.

If your sales forecast shows that you will not achieve 6,250 units sold until June, for the first half of the year you will be working at a loss.

The sooner you reach that magic number of units, the sooner your department is going to be working at a profit.

Naturally, this only shows the cost-effectiveness of the sales department. The accountants at head office are working things out in a different way. They're concerned about gross margin. Your budgeting therefore also has to take account of margins on the various product lines sold, even though the breakeven formula above doesn't take gross margin into account.

Always remember, your *organisation* gets to profitability quicker, if your sales people concentrate on sales of high gross-margin products/services.

Selling costs are often also divided into direct and indirect, as follows:

Direct Selling Costs – include the cost of calling by salespeople and managers on accounts and prospects, salaries, incentives, compensation and travel.

Indirect Costs – include supervision, sales office expenses, sales administration, training, marketing research and new product development.

Other costs often allocated against the sales department are advertising, sales promotion, transport and storage.

Although the last two items may not seem too important, bear in mind that some bright spark in accounts may change perfectly good (to you) transport and storage systems in order to save money – which changes could have a negative effect on your customers. Be aware!

There are many important **key ratios** which you can work out and use for control purposes once your budgeting has been done, e.g. average cost of sales call, average cost of obtaining new clients, etc.

All these can be calculated using computer spread sheets. If you don't know how to use a computer spread sheet program – learn!

C

Company Cars

Thirty years ago, the company car was practically a tax-free benefit. At that time, pretty well the only people to get company cars were salespeople, sales managers and directors.

In the intervening years, more and more employees have been given cars as perks of the job and the tax benefits have eroded away to almost nothing. Now, relatively junior management in personnel and accounts receive company cars and young men and women working in finance in the City receive high performance cars as part of their bonuses.

One of the enduring anomalies of British business is the fact that the best, most expensive and most luxurious company cars spend their entire time parked outside the company's head office. They probably do no more than three or four thousand miles a year on company business. Yes, I'm talking about directors' cars.

(You notice we still have directors' car parks. They're the ones nearest the main entrance of company HQ. They're there so the directors won't get wet if it's raining when they park. Does it rain more on directors than it does on other employees? Who says class is dying in British business?)

On the other hand, salespeople and sales managers, the people for whom a car is actually a tool of the job – just as much as a pen, a spanner, a desktop computer or a telephone – don't receive anywhere near the same standard of company car as directors. So, it is up to you as the sales manager to fight for your people. To get them the best car possible.

Of course, it's pushing it to think that you or your people can get the equivalent of directors' cars. But, bearing in mind that the annual average mileage for industrial salespeople is around 30,000 miles a year, (up to 40,000 for a sales manager), a good quality car which ensures comfort, safety and freedom from fatigue is an absolute must if your salespeople are to turn in consistently high sales performances.

Air conditioning is a must. Yes, there *are* hot days in this country. It does not create a great impression if your salespeople turn up at their customers' offices drenched in sweat.

So, if your company doesn't view salespeople's cars as essential tools of the job, you must educate them accordingly. Your entire focus must be on the best car for the salespeople to do their job. Considerations of status and reward come afterwards.

Following are some outline rules for the use of company cars. Whatever the rules are within your company, stick with them rigidly. Do not allow any of your salespeople to start bending the rules or abusing the privileges attached to the use of a company car. If one person gets an edge, like having a tow bar for a trailer or caravan, or fitting a 'virtual Dolby surround' stereo system, then the rest will want the same kind of treatment. Modifications to cars will also affect (usually adversely) the resale value of the car.

It will be your job to scrutinise and sign off salespeople's expenses, including car running costs. Watch out for petrol purchases on a Friday followed by more petrol purchases on the Monday – unless of course the salesperson is working for the company over the weekend. Salespeople (including you) should purchase their own petrol for private mileage at weekends.

Do not allow the salespeople to purchase sweets, cigarettes, newspapers and so on, on the same bill as the company petrol. When this happens, companies find themselves inadvertently reimbursing salespeople for their private purchases and, to add insult to injury, the Inland Revenue has been known to 'hit' the company for the tax benefit, it being easier to charge the company than the individuals.

Rules for the Use of Company Cars

Driving Licences and Authority to Drive Company Cars

(a)   The person must be in possession of a current driving licence and have the company's authority to drive one of its vehicles, which authority must be given by the company secretary.

(b)   The person's driving licence must have been produced for scrutiny by the company secretary, or in his absence, a director.

(c)   If at any time the driver's licence is endorsed or he is disqualified from driving, the company secretary must be informed immediately.

(d)   It is the responsibility of the driver of the vehicle to see that it is not driven by anyone other than authorised company employees. Special written permission must be obtained from the company secretary for the car to be used by any other driver not falling into this category.

Acceptance of Vehicle and Company Rules

At the time of taking over a company car, the company secretary will ask the driver to inspect the vehicle and agree its condition and to sign a form of receipt which will incorporate any existing faults, etc. Additionally all drivers will be asked to sign for a copy of the company's rules for the use of company cars and their signature will be taken as their acceptance of these rules.

If permission is given for a person other than the authorised driver to use the car, in addition to inspecting that person's driving licence, the company secretary must have a signature from that person acknowledging receipt of the company's rules for the use of company cars.

Fixtures, Fittings and Modifications

No fixtures such as aerials, roof racks, towing apparatus or stickers may be attached to company vehicles without prior written permission from the company secretary. When handing vehicles back to the company, such attachments must remain unless adequate rectification work is carried out professionally to restore the vehicle to its former condition.

No change or alterations may be made to the mechanical or structural specification as delivered of any company vehicle.

Warranty

When a new car is handed to a driver, a copy of the manufacturer's warranty is also presented. It is the driver's responsibility to ensure that any costs which may arise and which fall under the terms of the warranty are reported to the company secretary in advance of any work being carried out and if the driver cannot obtain free of charge repairs from a garage licensed by the manufacturer, no charges may be incurred without prior written permission from the company secretary. If any charges are incurred without following this rule, they must be borne by the driver since the manufacturer will not accept responsibility for work already carried out.

Cleaning and Maintenance

When a company car has been allocated to a particular driver, it is that person's responsibility to keep the car clean and to ensure that the vehicle is regularly serviced in accordance with the requirements laid down by the manufacturers and specified in the maintenance book of the particular model of car.

Unless contrary arrangements exist in writing between the company and the driver, the company will reimburse the driver for amounts spent on regular servicing provided a receipt is submitted to the company accompanied by a claim for reimbursement detailed on a company expense voucher.

Any other maintenance or repair work or replacement of parts including tyres must be approved in advance by the company secretary and reimbursement will only be made against production of an authorisation. Full details of the work required and the cost involved must be given.

Fuel, etc.

In addition to keeping the vehicle regularly serviced, it is the driver's responsibility to see that the oil and water levels, battery, brake and clutch fluids and tyre pressures are kept constantly in the correct state.

Petrol octane ratings, oil grades and all other fluids must conform to manufacturer's recommendations as laid down in the driver's handbook.

Unless contrary arrangements exist in writing between the company and the driver, the company will only reimburse the driver for petrol and oil used on company business. Claims must be submitted on an expense voucher signed by the individual and accompanied by receipted bills. All bills should be listed and a deduction shown for that part of the fuel attributable to private mileage.

No personal items may be shown on any bill covering petrol purchased for company use. Such items as newspapers, sweets, cigarettes, magazines and so on must be paid for separately by the sales person.

Garaging

The company will pay for garaging of the company car when, as a matter of course, high-cost company products are carried within the car. In all other cases, costs incurred by drivers for garaging cars must be their responsibility.

Fines

The company cannot, under any circumstances, accept responsibility for parking, driving or other fines incurred by drivers.

Insurance

(a) General

Motor vehicle insurance is expensive and annually getting more so. All vehicles used within the company are insured on a fleet basis which enables the company to enjoy a larger no-claim bonus than would be possible by insuring individual vehicles. However, this means that the accident record is calculated on a fleet aggregate, and it is incumbent upon every driver to exercise special care in respect of the vehicle within his or her control, otherwise he or she will incur expense which will affect the premium rating for all the cars used by the company.

(b) Premium

To keep the premium within reasonable limits, the company will agree with their insurers to accept a proportion of the costs of each claim, known as the excess. Provided the company driver is in no way to blame for the accident and the identity of the other party or parties involved is known, it is sometimes possible to recover some or all of this excess. It is emphasised, however, that any accident in which a company car is involved will probably cost the company a considerable amount of money at the time the repairs are carried out, and will also jeopardise their chances of avoiding an increase in premium when the insurance is due for renewal.

(c) Damage or Injury

The driver of any vehicle which is involved in an accident which causes damage or injury to any person, vehicle or animal is required to give his or her name and address, the name and address of the owner and the registration number of the vehicle and the name of his insurance company to any person having reasonable grounds for requiring such information. IT IS IMPORTANT THAT HE OR SHE GIVES NO FURTHER INFORMATION. If for some reason it is not possible to give this information at the time of the accident, the matter must be reported to the police as soon as possible AND WITHIN TWENTY-FOUR HOURS OF THE OCCURRENCE.

In addition, in the case of an accident involving injury to another person or to certain animals, the driver is responsible for notifying the police of the occurrence and must produce his or her insurance certificate to the police officer attending the accident or to any other person having reasonable grounds for seeing it. The accident must be reported at a police station or to a police officer within twenty-four hours. If the driver is not then able to produce the certificate, he or she must in any event produce it in person within five days after the accident to such police station as he or she may specify at the time of reporting the accident in the first place.

For security reasons, insurance certificates are kept by the company secretary. A facsimile of the certificate of insurance is provided with each vehicle however, and this will be renewed annually. All drivers should make sure that it is with the vehicle at all times. Replacement copies can be obtained from the company secretary's office if necessary.

(d) Loss

In the case of loss of a company vehicle, the police and the company secretary must be immediately informed. Full details of the contents of the car must also be given to the company secretary. If any contents are stolen from a company car, the police and the company secretary should be notified immediately.

Drivers should note particularly that only company property is insured by the company and they should make their own arrangements to cover personal effects.

All company cars should be kept locked when not in use and contents should be stored out of sight, preferably in the boot. If a car is stolen, the company is required to prove to the insurance company that there has been no negligence and therefore the company must hold the driver responsible in the event of negligence.

(e) Claims

It is a condition of the insurance policy that the insurers are notified of all accidents, even if apparently of no consequence. The driver must, therefore, as soon as possible after the accident, get from the company secretary an accident report form which must be completed and returned to the company secretary's office within twenty-four hours. All the information required on the form must be completed, and if necessary, the company secretary's office will give every assistance in its completion, but in any event the driver should note that whenever possible the following particulars should appear in the form:

(i) The name and address of the third party driver and the name and address of his or her insurers.

(ii) The names and addresses of all passengers in both the company car and the third party's vehicle.

(iii) Names and addresses of all witnesses. It will be of considerable assistance if statements can be obtained from all witnesses at the time of the accident. Experience shows that if these are not obtained at the time, their value is usually negligible after any interval of time.

(iv) Particulars of the police attending, i.e. name, number and division.

A detailed sketch must be provided showing the relative position of the vehicle(s) before and after the accident together with details of the roads in the vicinity, e.g. whether they are major or minor roads and as many relevant measurements as possible.

If the vehicle belonging to the company is undrivable, the driver is responsible for making adequate arrangements for the vehicle to be towed to a garage and the name and address of the garage where the vehicle can be inspected must be stated on the claim form.

UNDER NO CIRCUMSTANCES MAY REPAIRS BE PUT IN HAND UNTIL THE INSURANCE COMPANY HAS GIVEN ITS AGREEMENT. The company secretary will give the necessary authority.

An estimate of the repairs required to be carried out, showing details and cost of both labour and materials, must be obtained and sent to the company secretary's office as soon as possible.

A driver should not UNDER ANY CIRCUMSTANCES express any opinion one way or another on the degree of responsibility for the accident. The driver should just exchange the particulars mentioned in the Insurance (c) section, and nothing more.

Please note also that no statements should be made to the police without written permission from the company secretary. This is particularly important in cases involving death or injury and leading to an inquest or inquiry, as the driver will have to be legally represented and would not wish to prejudice his position in any way.

Seat Belts

Seat belts are fitted to all company cars. It is the law that drivers and ALL passengers should wear them on ALL journeys.

Road Fund Licence

The road fund licence for each vehicle will automatically be renewed when due, but in the event that the new licence is not received by the driver within fourteen days of the previous licence's expiry date, the company secretary should be immediately notified by telephone.

Travel Overseas

No company vehicle may be taken out of the country without written permission from the company secretary or managing director of the company.

The company's insurance policy covers the use of their vehicles in Great Britain, Northern Ireland, the Isle of Man and the Channel Islands.

Before travelling with the vehicle anywhere else, the driver, having first obtained permission, must inform the company secretary at least 21 days beforehand, giving a list of the countries to be visited and the relevant dates. An insurance certificate (green card) will then be issued which must accompany the vehicle.

On return to England, this certificate should be returned to the company secretary for cancellation.

Unless the journey is on approved company business, the cost of the green card will be charged to the driver and must be paid before the journey commences.

General Security

At all times when leaving the vehicle unattended, the driver must ensure that all windows are closed, the ignition key removed and the vehicle securely locked.

Personal Baggage

Articles of any kind carried in the vehicle and not the property of the company are at the risk of the owner of the property and the company accepts no responsibility for such property.

Permitted Use

Subject to the restrictions already stipulated, private vehicles may only be used for social, domestic and pleasure purposes and used for the business of the company, excluding the carriage of passengers for hire or reward. Company vehicles may not be used for any type of motoring sport, including racing, rallying or pace making, whether on the public highway or on private land.

Commercial vehicles may only be used in connection with the company's business.

Priority Use

The company reserves the right to take back any car at any time should an occasion arise where the company has an imperative need for the vehicle.

Credit Control

A sale is not a sale until the order form is signed – right? Wrong. A sale is not a sale until it is paid for.

The sales department should be made aware by the accounts department of late payments by customers. Credit control should not be allowed to dun clients for late payment until you have been told. After all, your department got the order in the first place, and it is possible that you or one of your salespeople can do something about the problem. Perhaps even turn it into a selling opportunity.

On the flip side, it would be nice to compliment customers when they regularly pay on time. However, the problem is that, if the client company's Financial Director gets to know about on-time payments, he or she may decide to slow them up.

It is the *salesperson's* responsibility to secure payment for his or her orders.

This cannot be delegated to Credit Control – nor is abdication permissible.

The salesperson should agree the terms of payment personally with the customer and use this agreement as the basis for any necessary follow-up. Without such an obligation to honour the agreement, the customer will never help you get paid.

The *objective* of Credit Control is *not* to get up the customer's nose. It is to get the customer to pay quicker.

Thus the customer has to be made *happy*, not miserable.

Try giving your computer its own identity and getting it to send out its own letter with the overdue statement. See the example opposite.

Dear Customer

My name is Henry. I'm the Harcros Eastern Region computer.

Part of my job is to draw your attention to the overdue balance on the attached statement.

So far, only you and I know that this balance is overdue, but in seven days' time, I am programmed to tell the credit controller.

Why should we involve him?

Yours truly

Henry

SURVEY ON CREDIT CONTROL
(Survey conducted by Alex Lawrie)

Survey sample: 800+ businesses, 73% under 20 employees, 51% turnover below £1/2m, 30% more than £1m

HOW MUCH TIME IS SPENT ON CREDIT CONTROL AND CASH FLOW ISSUES?

Too little	11.8%
Too much	22.9%
About right	65.3%

HOW MANY TELEPHONE CALLS ARE MADE EACH WEEK CHASING DEBTORS?

Less than 10 calls per week	70%
0-5 calls	48.8%
6-10 calls	21.9%
11-20 calls	14.1%
20+ calls	15.2%

HOW MANY DAYS LATE ARE CUSTOMERS PAYING?

30-40 days late	34.4%
41-50 days late	28.3%
51-60 days late	21.8%
61-70 days late	11.5%
70+ days late	4.1%

Average time before account is settled – 70 days

HOW DO YOU FEEL ABOUT DISCOUNTS FOR EARLY PAYMENT?

Inevitable but costly	17.6%
Would not consider	46.2%
Approve of discounts	36.2%

HOW OFTEN DO YOU CREDIT CHECK YOUR CUSTOMERS?

Once upon opening account	47.7%
Never	26.7%
Regularly	19.7%
Once a year	5.9%

Criteria for Ordering

If you were to conduct a survey of all your customers, in which you asked them, 'when you made the decision to choose us as your supplier for these products/services, what factors did you consider in deciding we were your best bet? What were your criteria for ordering in this case?' – what kinds of lists of your customers' criteria for ordering do you think you would get? And if you processed all these lists of CFOs through your computer to come up with ONE list which typified ALL your customers' CFOs, what would this CFO list say?

It would be a VERY valuable sales aid – one that could be used in every conceivable sales situation as a hundred or a thousand cumulative testimonials. A veritable gold brick which should be added to every quotation that your company sends out.

Better than that, a CFO list is a most effective way to sell your higher price. That's why it begins with 'PRICE - best value for money', and then continues with the longest possible list that you can put together of the things important to your customers, where you are BETTER – or just as good as – your competitors. ('Just as good as' works because when you use the CFO list, your competitors aren't there to argue – and your customer won't know enough to argue!)

Your long list under 'PRICE' is what you (or your customers) see clearly is what they will be getting for the little extra, the difference in price between you and the competition they are looking at. And those competitors won't even be using a CFO list!

Better than that, you don't have to conduct a survey of all your customers in order to produce a CFO list. You can do it in an hour with your salespeople and a few flipcharts, because your salespeople should know why your customers decided to buy from you. So, let's get it all out of them and onto the flipcharts.

RESULTS OF A ONE HOUR
'WHY DO PEOPLE BUY FROM US?'
SESSION
led by John Fenton for Oddbins Ltd,
Corporate Business Sales Team.

(This list is at random, with no specific order, just as it was written on flipcharts during the session. It is the starting point when you are building your own CFO list. As an exercise, get your salespeople to construct a CFO list from all this random data.)

- One *local* telephone call for EVERYTHING. And the local people know everything about you – as a Corporate customer.

- The product range is EXCITING, INNOVATIVE – VERY DIFFERENT from your bog-standard wine merchant.

- We are the market leaders, the trend setters.

- We make our *customers* stand out and be different.

- We can design and produce your Wine Lists, blackboards, organise tastings, educate your staff. Any time you like, you can visit your local branch for tasting.

- You share in our reputation and success for the most exciting 'Bin-Ends' which you can regularly add to your on-going Wine-List to tickle your customers' fancy.

- Big groups can run a National Account on a local basis.

- We talk your language.

- We are very nice people to do business with. We'll make you feel good, not make you feel miserable.

- We run extensive gift vouchers, Christmas boxes and incentive scheme services for your customers or staff.

- *Your* needs are our concern. We do not put obstacles in the way – we make things happen.

- We *love* joint ventures.

- We can give you a better class of customer – the people who spend more. When your customers know you use Oddbins, other things will happen.

- Why? – Because we are 'WHICH?' magazine's National High Street Chain Wine Merchant of the Year – and have been for the last three years.

- We have been the International Wine Challenge 'Wine Merchant of the Year' for five consecutive years. We didn't win last year, because they didn't allow us to enter. 'Give someone else a chance', they said.

- Our annual Wine Fairs are major events in the international wine business. All our new Corporate customers are invited, free.

- You will never find such enthusiasm and dedication anywhere else.

- We care. We believe.

- All our Corporate Account Managers are wine experts – and there is nothing in our range that they wouldn't happily drink themselves.

- Our branch is like having your own cellar, but just around the corner. With your bog-standard wine merchant, you might wait a week and can only contact them 9am to 5pm, Monday to Friday. With us, you can get your emergency supplies 10am to 10pm Monday to Saturday and 12pm to 3pm on Sunday.

- We trust you! You get corporate prices from the word go.

- Our range is so wide that we can give two or three customers in the same area a totally different but equally exciting Wine List.

- You can buy a single bottle or 100 cases – the only factor is a £50 minimum order value.

- You get full Sale or Return facilities and a glasses service for functions.

Your Criteria for Ordering Training

Your random list on the flipcharts can then be developed into a 'gold brick' CFO list, like the following:

Here are the top twelve reasons why 8,000+ British based businesses decided on John Fenton Training. How many of these twelve would be included in your Criteria for Ordering, when you are looking for an outside training organisation to improve the performance of your people.

PRICE

If you had a heart problem and had to buy yourself a pacemaker, would you look around for the lowest price? It's the same with training. Very few businesses buy training on the basis of lowest price. When you're looking for performance improvement, you look for the best, not the cheapest. Customers buy training on the basis of best return on their investment.

TOP PRIORITY SUBJECTS

John Fenton master classes focus on a small number of top priority subjects and do the very best job that can be done. There are no 'maybe' areas, just highly practical training based upon other people's most successful ways of doing the job. John Fenton's genius for getting to the nub of the matter shines through every time.

RESULTS FAST

Customers want to see results from their training investment now. Improved performance, more positive attitude, more sales, more profits. Every John Fenton master class focuses on the fastest possible results.

MINIMUM TIME OFF THE JOB

Few customers appreciate having their key people away from the job on a training course for an entire week, where a good half of the fee goes to pay the hotel accommodation and evening meal costs and has no training value – *and* they also lose a whole week's 'production'. John Fenton master classes achieve in *one day* the same amount of performance improvement that most other training organisations take three days or more to achieve.

MONEY BACK GUARANTEE

John Fenton master class customers just can't lose, because everything is backed up with a 'no quibble' full refund guarantee if the customer is not fully satisfied. Few training organisations are this confident about their product quality.

MAXIMUM FEEL GOOD FACTOR

Customers want their people to feel good about attending a training course. With volunteers, there is never a problem, but people who are 'sent' without any option can arrive with a negative attitude, stay with a closed mind all day and not learn a thing. John Fenton master classes are not training courses, they are *master classes*. Better than that, they are master classes developed by John Fenton, the man who has led Britain's National Sales Convention since 1983. The venues are top notch. The master class *manuals* are 150 pages of really practical, useable *quality*. Delegates work with unique *on-the-job selling tools*, like the John Fenton *story board* on Professional Tele-Selling and Winning Appointments, the PPM system on Selling and the Motivation File on Sales Management. It all adds up to *maximum feel good factor* on arrival and throughout the day. Open minds, ready to learn, from the very start. Your delegates are treated as VIPs.

LOCAL VENUES – TOP FLIGHT TRAINERS

Meeting customers' expectations has brought about the JFTI master class Licensing network. Before John Fenton began recruiting and training his Licensees, all delegates attended master classes at the JFTI headquarters, near Stratford-upon-Avon, a pretty long trek for many for a one-day event. Now customers can send their people to the nearest, most convenient venue for their master classes, confident that the standard of training will be equal to master classes led by John Fenton himself.

SIT IN AND SEE FOR YOURSELF

Notwithstanding the money back guarantee, managers often want to check out the relevance of the training before sending their troops. Few training organisations offer this facility. John Fenton Training does. The normal format is for the manager to join the master class at mid-morning coffee break and sit in until lunchtime, discussing any specific questions over lunch with the Trainer who is leading the master class. This facility is available at all venues.

TAILOR MADE TRAINING

Customers can reserve a master class date and venue all to themselves and have the open master class tailor-made to suit only their requirements. The costs of this are normally no more than sending the same number of delegates to an open master class, subject to a minimum of 8 delegates.

Completely different tailor-mades can be designed and run the same way or at a venue of the customer's choice.

GREAT ON-GOING CUSTOMER CARE

JFT's local Trainer will ring you regularly to check on the progress of each and every delegate you send to the master classes and to provide on-going help and advice on your future training needs. John Fenton customers feel part of a large and rapidly growing family. Another kind of Feel Good Factor.

IMPECCABLE TRACK RECORD

The best people to testify to the effectiveness of a training organisation are its customers. Every delegate assessment form is on file, as is every testimonial letter received from a customer – all open for inspection.

THE HEINEKEN FACTOR

John Fenton Training reaches the parts that other training doesn't reach.

There follow four more examples of CFO lists which have been developed for businesses by John Fenton.

Don't re-invent the wheel – steal and use anything that fits the customers' CFO for your business.

Your Criteria for Ordering

These eight criteria are what we at Harcros work hard to provide our customers. How many of these eight are important to YOU when you are choosing a supplier?

1. PRICE — Best value for money

2. DELIVERY — Keeping promises...and able to help you out with last minute requirements.

3. QUALITY — Meets your specifications...and KEEPS meeting them.

4. COMPETENCE — Technical and commercial. Gets your orders right, sorts out the paperwork right, deals with "returns" without delay

5. RANGE — One stop buying. Everything you need from one supplier.

6. SERVICE RESPONSE — Quick and effective with no delays which cost you money in lost production.

7. COMMUNICATIONS — Easy to do business with. Easy to get hold of people you want to talk to.

8. PHILOSOPHY — Puts the customer first, not its own problems.

HARCROS

Timber & Building Supplies

The Tennant Rubber Co Ltd

These are the principle reasons our customers buy from us.

How many of these reasons feature on YOUR list of factors that you look for when you are choosing suppliers?

PRICE	We do our best to give you the very best value for money
QUALITY	Both in product and specification
RELIABILITY	Systems conformance with BS5750
LEADING EDGE SUPPLIER	We keep you informed of new product development which gives you even better value for money
ONE STOP SHOPPING	Around 1700 products in stock - plus we do specials FAST
EASY TO DO BUSINESS WITH	Competent, knowledgeable staff who put YOU first
PROBLEM SOLVING	And they are **technically** competent too
WE DO THE LEG WORK	If we haven't got it we'll find it for you
NICE PEOPLE	You feel comfortable and secure with our staff
COMPANY PHILOSOPHY	**OUR AIM IS TO SELL GOODS THAT DON'T COME BACK TO PEOPLE WHO DO**

James Dubois & Co.

Chartered Accountants
and Registered Auditor

5 Lynwood Road
Epsom, Surrey
KT17 4LF

Phone: 01372 745129
Fax: 01372 745138

CLIENT REASONS *These are some of the reasons most of our clients deal with us:*	On Scale of 1-5 Your Rating
PRICE — *We give you real value for money. This means we hardly ever lose a client because of price.*	
RELIABILITY — *We produce your work when YOU need it.*	
QUALITY — *Our aim is to give you the best - Total Quality Management for a quality service.*	
RESPONSE — *We're quick and efficient; delays cost you money and cause inconvenience.*	
PROBLEM SOLVING — *We're here to solve your problems.*	
COMPETENCE — *We get your work right with the minimum disruption to your business.*	
PERSONAL SERVICE — *Our people are there when you need to talk or meet with them. We're convenient; we all know the clients and we react quickly.*	
HELPFUL — *When we ask our clients why they deal with us, they say: "Because we like the people; they know their stuff; they're helpful; they're happy; they try harder".*	
PHILOSOPHY — *We put our clients FIRST. We CARE.*	

VAT No: 564 099907

Registered to carry out Audit work and Authorised to carry on Investment Business by the Institute of Chartered Accountants in England & Wales

James Dubois FCA

WHY PEOPLE BUY FROM

These are the top twelve reasons why people have chosen to buy from us.
How many of these reasons are important to YOU?

PRICE Best all round value for your money.

QUALITY ISO9001 (BS 5750 Part 1) backed with our own warranty, both as a manufacturer and as a supplier.
Approvals include WRC, CE Mark and UL.

DELIVERY We keep our promises.

RELIABILITY A fully documented history of proven performance, minimum down time and longest working life.

SERVICE Pre-sales, after-sales, technical and commercial. The largest service team in the business. Our goal as a company is to have customer service that is not just the best, but is legendary.

REPUTATION Almost a century of continual supply of the best equipment and service available to the catering industry.

RANGE Comprehensive, to meet most needs.

TRAINING Nobody does it better - initial, on-going and whenever and wherever you need it.

EASY TO DO BUSINESS WITH National coverage; good communications; minimum hassle. People who understand YOUR business. Personal service from local people.

NICE PEOPLE Time after time, when we ask customers why they prefer to buy from Hobart Still, they say "Because we like the people. They know their stuff; they're helpful; they're happy and they try harder.

FINANCE We help you to find the money to buy, lease or rent the best equipment.

WE CARE How our customers feel about us today decides our success or failure tomorrow.

Customer Records

The vast majority of people in your company never ever get to see the company's customers. Their knowledge of customers comes through customer records. The more comprehensive and detailed you make these records, the closer the company gets to its customers.

Detailed, comprehensive customer records are one of your company's most valuable assets.

For the sales department, they are priceless. Treat them as such. Maintain their security. Always remember that an unscrupulous competitor would give a lot to see your records.

If they are not computerised, get them computerised. Once records are on computer, so much more information can be included, and the entire customer record base can be searched in seconds. That's one of the great things about computers – they don't need an alphabet. They search at virtually the speed of light. An ordinary desktop computer can do a keyword search on 50,000 words almost as quickly as you can write, 'fifty thousand words'.

So, apart from including the obvious in your records – name and address of the company, contacts' names and positions, product lines and value sold per call, etc., computerised records can also include considerable detail about the company, such as its type of business, size by turnover and number of employees, its major product lines and so on.

Your records can also include how the customer company uses your products (you need to standardise the terminology for this) and of course your sales people can put in the time and date of their next intended sales call.

On computer, all this information is live and accessible. Your customer records are no longer stuffed into filing cabinets and never looked at again. Just a couple of strokes of the keyboard and you'll see which customers all your salespeople intend calling on a week next Tuesday.

Or, supposing the product or service you sell is being used by 80% of your customers for one application and by 20% for another. A data search on your customer records could reveal that the secondary application is growing fast. Why? What potential markets does this open for your product or service? What new products or services could you be developing to meet this growing use? Get the picture?

Customer records are the lifeblood of the entire company. But only when they're used, reviewed, analysed and searched.

But note that a *File* is still the best for those occasions when the salesperson gets face-to-face with the customer. The File itself only costs 20 pence. The call – any kind of call – will cost between £40 and £80 or more. Why spoil the ship for a ha'p'orth of tar? You cannot make a Professional First Impression with a computer.

AND – *all records must be retrieved* from a salesperson who leaves – it is the law, anyway, and you need everything to give to the replacement.

Have a *standardised* Customer Record format. Never let the salespeople devise their own individually. (And even if they do – and pay for them themselves – they are still, by law, Company property).

See example Standardised Customer Record File on next four pages.

CUSTOMER

CODE

"YOU NEVER GET A SECOND CHANCE
TO MAKE A FIRST IMPRESSION"
The John Fenton Training Customer Care File ©1997

WHAT THE CUSTOMERS SAY

"Since attending the Quoting Master Class on 7th October I have maintained a 100% success record in seeking and securing new contract."
Martin Sewell, Chairman
Marketing Initiatives Limited

"I enclose the two forms which I started to use the day after attending your Master Class. On the first major client I have quoted since then, they were a resounding success. They became so fired up with our enthusiasm for helping them that we never actually got back to discussing the price at all!"
James Dubois PCA
James Dubois & Co, Chartered Accountants

"VERY good. Refreshed old ideas and gave a valued injection of Fentonisms. All parts were relevant."
Alan Pearson, Managing Director,
Thurmon (UK) Ltd.

"MAGIC! Very helpful, idea packed, plenty of things every delegate could apply at the very next opportunity to increase business."
William Bryden-Smith
Technology Industries

"Mind blowing!"
Phil Cooper, Branch Manager
Abbots Packaging Ltd.

"The most valuable input on motivation I have ever received. All of SIBMAP I found relevant to my business, professional and detailed. Now I can really get to work."
Richard Lamb, Managing Director
Ultra-Pro Ltd

CALL RECORD				
DATE	WHAT HAPPENED	OBJECTIVE FOR NEXT CALL	DATE	FIRM APPOINT MADE / TIME

CUSTOMER		
ADDRESS		
POST CODE	TELEPHONE No E MAIL ADDRESS	FAX No WWW
NATURE OF BUSINESS		
PARENT/SUBSIDIARIES		
SIZE (No OF STAFF)	TURNOVER	CREDIT LIMIT
TERMS OF PAYMENT	AGREED WITH	DATE AGREED

DECISION MAKING UNIT (DMU)

Size of company (Number of employees)	Average number of decision influencers	Average number of influencers who talk to Salespeople
less than 200	3.43	1.72
201 to 400	4.85	1.75
401 to 1,000	5.81	1.90
more than 1,001	6.50	1.65

Source: Financial Times "HOW BRITISH INDUSTRY BUYS"

STRUCTURE OF CUSTOMER'S DMU (NUMBER PERSONNEL AS BELOW)

DMU PERSONNEL	FULL NAME OR INITIALS	JOB TITLE	TEL EXT	BEST DAY AND TIME	LUNCH HABITS	AGREED CALL FREQUENCY	APPOINT OR PCARD	BIRTH DAY	OBJECTIVE PRIORITIES
1									
2									
3									
4									
5									
6									
7									
8									

CUSTOMER'S OBJECTIVES

These are the objectives most of our customers want to achieve from using our training services, which of them are YOUR objectives?

PRIORITY ORDER

INCREASE	Orders, Turnover, Profits, Call Rate, Appointments, Number of DMU contacts seen, Feel Good Factor, Market Share	
IMPROVE	Cash Flow, Presentation, Market Perception, First Impressions, Management Performance, Sales Performance, Staff Motivation, Effectiveness, Negotiating Skills, Closing Skills	
REDUCE	Selling Costs, Staff Turnover, Cost of Recruitment, Travelling Time, Mileage, Wasted Calls, Borrowings, Risk of choosing the wrong training, Calls to Quotes Ratios, Quotes to Order Ratios, Discounts	
SAVE	Time and Money	
GAIN	Up to 50% grant from the TEC, New Customers, Respect, Peace of Mind, CPE and Units of Competence for your MBA	
Any Other Objectives		

CRITERIA FOR ORDERING (CFO)

Here are the top twelve reasons why 7000 plus British based businesses decided on John Fenton Training.

How many of these twelve would be included in **YOUR** Criteria for Ordering, when you are looking for an outside training organisation to improve the performance of your people?

PRICE
Very few businesses buy training on the basis of lowest price. When they are looking for performance improvement, they look for the BEST value for their money.

TOP PRIORITY SUBJECTS
John Fenton Master Classes focus on a small number of top priority subjects and do the very best job that can be done. Highly practical training based upon other people's most successful ways of doing the job.

RESULTS FAST
Customers want to see results from their training investment NOW. Improved performance, more positive attitude, more sales, more profits. Every John Fenton Master Class focuses on the fastest possible results.

MINIMUM TIME OFF THE JOB
John Fenton Master Classes achieve in ONE DAY the same amount of performance improvement that most other training organisations take three days or more to achieve.

MONEY BACK GUARANTEE
Everything is backed up with a "no quibble" full refund guarantee if the customer is not fully satisfied.

MAXIMUM FEEL GOOD FACTOR
Your delegates attend MASTER CLASSES, not training courses, They are treated as VIPs. The venues are top notch. The Master Class MANUALS are 150 pages of really practical, useable QUALITY. Delegates work with unique hands on tools, like the STORY BOARD on Tele-Selling, the PPM System on Selling and the SIMBAP master plan. No other trainers have these.

LOCAL VENUES TOP FLIGHT TRAINERS
Customers can send their people to the nearest, most convenient venue, confident that the standard of training will be equal to Master Classes led by John Fenton himself.

SIT IN AND SEE FOR YOURSELF
Few training organisations offer this facility. JFT does.

PREVIEW DAYS
Every six months at most venues, you can preview all the forthcoming Master Classes in one day.

TAILOR MADE TRAINING
Customers can reserve a date and venue all to themselves and have the Master Class tailor-made to suit only their requirements.

GREAT ON-GOING CUSTOMER CARE
Your local JFT Principal Trainer will ring you regularly to check on the progress of every delegate you send to the Master Classes and to provide on-going help and advice on your future training needs.

IMPECCABLE TRACK RECORD
Every delegate assessment form is on file; every testimonial letter received from a customer - all open for inspection.

YOUR ASSESSMENT OF US (MAXIMUM 10)			COMPETITOR 1		COMPETITOR 2	
WEIGHT	RATING	W x R	R	WxR	R	WxR

REFERRALS

	Does the customer know of anyone else who could use our products/services?	Would the customer telephone the referral on our behalf, as an introduction?
NAME COMPANY ADDRESS	JOB TITLE	BUSINESS, PROBLEMS, SUPPLIERS, ETC
POST CODE	TELEPHONE	
NAME COMPANY ADDRESS	JOB TITLE	BUSINESS, PROBLEMS, SUPPLIERS, ETC
POST CODE	TELEPHONE	
NAME COMPANY ADDRESS	JOB TITLE	BUSINESS, PROBLEMS, SUPPLIERS, ETC
POST CODE	TELEPHONE	
NAME COMPANY ADDRESS	JOB TITLE	BUSINESS, PROBLEMS, SUPPLIERS, ETC
POST CODE	TELEPHONE	
NAME COMPANY ADDRESS	JOB TITLE	BUSINESS, PROBLEMS, SUPPLIERS, ETC
POST CODE	TELEPHONE	

"By the way, before I go, do you know anyone else who might be interested in what we do?"

"What do they do?"

"Who do they buy from now, do you know?"

"Any problems?"

"Who's your opposite number over there?"

"Do you know him/her well?"

"Er, I wonder, I know it's a bit of a cheek, but you know how difficult it is cold, as an unknown quantity. Would you mind giving them a ring for me, while I'm here, to oil the wheels, so to speak?"

"How are we doing, by the way?"

"Are we living up to what you expected from us as a supplier?"

"Would you write to my managing director and tell him?"

D

Decision Making

Most of us hate making decisions. We are aware of our own frailties – we're never sure if we've got it right – and anyway, we remember the bad decisions we've made in the past.

Try remembering the good decisions for a change. You must have made some – or you wouldn't be where you are today.

The problem with making decisions is that you're under the spotlight. Everyone else can see you've got the ball and they're fascinated to see what you do with it. Some may even want to see you drop it.

You've heard the rule that *any decision is better than no decision*. Of course that's true. However, it does give an impression of panic. And that is the last thing you want in decision making. Panic is subjective.

All decisions should be *objective*. Or as objective as we can possibly make them.

Most decisions fall into two overlapping areas – operational and human. Of course, most operational decisions also affect people. However, the general principles of decision making apply to both.

General Principles of Decision Making

Be objective

This is easier said than done. None of us is totally objective. The man or woman who tells you that he or she is always completely objective is making a highly subjective statement.

If you have subjective feelings about a decision, identify them and try to put them on one side.

Get all the facts

Again, this is the counsel of perfection. Many people use the excuse of waiting to get *all* the facts in order *not* to make a decision. So, remember the 80/20 rule. You can probably assemble 80% of the facts in a short time. It may take too long to get the other 20%. And remember, with many decisions, time is of the essence.

Procrastination is a waste of time. Don't waste time trying to get all the facts. You'll never get all the facts – and even if you do, you won't know you've got them all.

Define the Problem

With as many of the facts to hand as possible, define the problem by *writing it down*. Keep writing it down, honing and refining it until you're pretty sure you have the specific – the real (as opposed to the apparent) problem – defined in all its parts. This means hard mental effort.

Analyse the problem into its constituent parts

What may at first have seemed a simple problem may have an impact on other areas. Try breaking it down. It may be that you need to make a few minor decisions rather than one big one.

Identify the solution(s)

Once you've got the actual problem written down, it is often fairly obvious what the solution should be. However, write down all possible solutions, including their possible or potential impact on other areas or departments. The best solution for you or your department may not be the best solution for the company as a whole.

Also, as you write down possible solutions, take into account not only the best solution but also the one that is *likely to succeed*. They are not always the same thing.

Decide and Do It

Once you've written down the best solution, decide on it and *do it*. Be brave, be incisive. That's what they're paying you for.

But, you say, what if I'm wrong?

So what? You're not God are you? *Change it – and fast!*

If the decision turns out to have been wrong or not the best one when viewed with hindsight – go through the process you followed. If you can honestly say that you followed the process right through but things still went wrong, then there's no need to whip yourself. Things happen. Maybe events you couldn't foresee affected the outcome of your decision.

If, however, you didn't follow the process, or if you rushed it, or took too long, or didn't put things down on paper, then learn the lesson for the next time – and move on. Don't dwell on it.

People Problems

All the above also relates to decisions about people. However, there is going to be a lot more subjectivity related to problems with people – including your own.

Again, get the facts, which means getting both sides of the story. As far as possible, forget your own prejudices and dislikes.

Discount all the adjectives people use about each other. He/she is selfish, belligerent, sexist, rude, dishonest and so on.

Where possible, get at the facts by checking on records.

Don't jump to conclusions and always check company policies when it comes to people problems.

When you finally come to a decision, take it bravely. Boldness and being fair is always praiseworthy

Many decisions have been made before. Not exactly the same perhaps, but close enough to provide some kind of guide line. That's what case studies at management schools are all about – past decisions and how they turned out.

Check around in the company. Has a similar problem been encountered before? If so, what was the decision? How did it turn out?

If you're dealing with a people problem, talk to someone outside the company who doesn't know the history or the people. Put it to them objectively. (Try your spouse or your partner. They like to be involved and it's good to value their judgement). Listen to their views. Often they see something glaringly obvious which you've missed because you're too close to the problem.

THE AGE-OLD CONFLICT

.
.
.

<u>Salespeople</u> judge themselves
by what they feel
capable of doing.

.
.

<u>Managers</u> judge them
by what they have
already done.

Direct Mail

Any company that can sell a high-unit-priced product to a discrete market that can be accurately accessed by direct mail, is streets ahead of competitors who have to sell to a larger market using general advertising. In fact, the spend on direct mail in the United States is more than the entire advertising spend (above and below the line) in the UK.

Good direct mail campaigns should generate sales leads for your sales force, ideally uncovering parts of the market that they haven't been able to reach before.

Use direct mail where you can, but employ specialist direct mail agencies. Shop around. As with everything in life, some are excellent, some are hopeless.

There are nine essential criteria in direct mail:

1. Envelope and Letterhead

The envelope must create a good impression. Don't make it look like a circular letter. If the mailing is small enough, have a clerk or outside worker stick stamps on the envelopes. Don't use your company letterheading in the direct mail shot. Create a new one, especially for that particular mailing.

2. Folding

The enclosed contents should emerge from the envelope in the way you want them to be read. It may seem a small point but it isn't. How often have you opened a mailshot which seems nothing but clutter?

3. Targeting

Many shots can be targeted to *individually named* potential customers. Many mailing lists available to rent or purchase are regularly updated with customer names. Computerised and laser technology can incorporate names into various places in the mailshot. Naturally, if you mailshot your existing customers, you can use names and other appropriate details that you know about them from your records.

Have the letter (which, in direct mail terms is the sales pitch) written by an experienced copy writer – under your direction. Make sure the copywriter is aware of the everyday technical language your market uses.

4. AIDA

Follow the *Attention, Interest, Desire, Action* format recommend in Advertising. Think of something that gains the recipient's attention and interest the moment the envelope is opened. This can be in the letter and also in the enclosure(s).

5. Proposition

This is mainly in the letter. Offer the recipient something to their advantage.

6. Weight

At the moment the Post Office allows 60g for a first or second class letter before an increase to the next postage rate. If possible, enclose material up to 59g, including the envelope, so that you maximise on the permitted weight. In direct mail, if the letter is the proposition, the enclosures are the product. This is where you incorporate pictures, testimonials etc., showing the emotional appeal of the product.

7. Credibility

Some direct mail campaigns fail because their originators weren't quite sure what they were selling. Is your direct mail shot selling the product directly – or is it selling the chance to be sold by one of your salespeople. You must know. Once you know, generate the desire to that end.

8. References

Third party references, particularly if you can use one of your existing customers, are a great aid to selling. Enclose testimonials and references wherever you can.

9. Action

(See under 'coupons' in Advertising) Make it easy for the recipient to respond – make it absolutely imperative that they do so – and make it **free**. Use a *Free Post* facility and/or a free 0800 telephone number.

50% MORE RESPONSE!

If you enclose a *fax response sheet* with your mail shot, personalised or not, you'll get a 50% better response, according to:
  (1) Halcyon Direct
  (2) Leonard, Holmes, Maclean

Samples of their fax response sheets follow:

HALCYON
DIRECT ▶

FAX REPLY SERVICE

TO: **Halcyon Direct Sales Department**
FAX Number: **01932 354846**

❑   Please call me to discuss the Arpeggio Remote
Ethernet ISDN Bridge

❑   Please call me to discuss corporate and quantity
discounts available on Arpeggio Bridge

❑   Please call me to discuss the 2100 CCT LAN
Certification and Troubleshooting Tool

❑   Please call me to arrange a free on-site
demonstration of the 2100 CCT LAN Certification
and Troubleshooting Tool

❑   Please call me to discuss my other data
communications and network requirements

Name...
Position ....
Company...
Address ....
....
....
....
Telephone ....FAX ....

Facsimile Transmission Cover Sheet

To:

Company:	Leonard, Holmes, Maclean
Phone:	01908 690880
Fax:	01908 670013

From:	**Andrew Gill**
Title:	**Marketing Director**
Company:	Glenigan Ltd
Phone:	
Fax:	

Pages including this: _____

Date: __/__/__

Please send me further information on the notebook PC offer ☐

Please send me my *FREE*

3.5" demonstration diskette ☐

5.25" demonstration diskette ☐

Additional information on Interact Direct ☐

Fax your requirements back on 01908 670013

Discounts

It's very easy to sell prices. Actually, if the Discount is big enough, it isn't selling, it's taking orders. The only problem is, the salesperson's company goes bust.

Profit margins must be maintained. Far too many salespeople are brainwashed into believing that Price is the only thing that matters. There are other things that are just as important, like quality, reliability, delivery, superior performance, and after-sales service.

If profit is not maintained, all these other things cannot be maintained either. They all have to be paid for.

Profit is the thing that should matter to salespeople, not turnover. Target and remuneration should be set according to profitability. Then they'd stop giving so many Discounts away.

The Discount – if it is necessary at all – should be the last thing the Salesman mentions to a customer, not the first.

Take a particular case: a salesperson is required to sell £100,000 worth of a product, with a gross profit margin of 15 per cent.

If he sells the £100,000 worth at list price, his contribution to his company's profits is £15,000. If, on the other hand, he sells the £100,000 worth at a 5 per cent discount, his contribution is only £10,000.

To get his contribution back up to the budgeted £15,000 profit, he will have to sell a further £50,000 worth of the product at a 5 per cent discount, or a further £33,400 worth at list price.

Was it really worth giving that 5 per cent away?

Non-Price-Sensitive Products/Services Never Get Discounted

How many products or services do we sell that are not price sensitive – i.e. where within reason, we could change the price up or down and it wouldn't make any difference to the volume of that product or service we actually sold?

Let's get our thinking caps on, sales team, and re-assess our range in this completely different way.

If we come up with anything, we'll consider putting up the price of it, *for the sheer hell of it*, by 10%.

What Harcros Timber & Building Supplies Did

They had 84,000 different products, of which 12,000 were non-price sensitive. Their 250 Branch managers were ordered to put the prices up on all 12,000 by a minimum 5%, to a maximum 15%, at their discretion. The result – an average price increase of 10.5% across the 12,000 n-p-s products, with *no loss of sales*. This equates to a 1.5% across the board price increase, *just for the hell of it*, with no change in Sales, Cost of Sales or Operating Costs, i.e. 1.5% extra NPBT. And no discounts.

E

Exhibitions

Exhibiting – Why it's still a Good Bet

There is still nothing to compare with a stand at a trade exhibition for launching a business and its products or services towards new customers, new contacts and new markets – providing that the stand itself is properly designed, the products are properly displayed, the stand manning staff perform properly and the inquiries are logged properly.

90% of businesses that exhibit still get at least two of these four provisos wrong – and pour their exhibition budget money down the drain.

It's why quite a few past exhibitors have been heard to comment unfavourably about the 'sport'. A recent survey quoted exhibitors as saying things like 'Stand space costs £100 a square metre, more than five times the cost of a first class hotel, but without a bed, bath, loo and colour TV. The stand itself costs about the same again!' and 'I'd rather increase coverage by other means without shows. Costs are becoming prohibitive' and 'In no other activity do managers leave themselves so exposed.'

So why are exhibitions good for some businesses and bad for others?

The answer is that exhibitions should be good for every kind of business. It's the approach to exhibiting and the way an exhibition cuts right across all departmental boundaries within the business, that gives senior executives a jaundiced opinion of this key element in sales promotion.

Compare the Costs with the Alternatives

One big problem is that businesses tend to look at the cost of an exhibition stand in isolation. They rarely compare the costs with alternative ways to generate the same amount of orders or enquiries.

Let me give you an example. If you were head of a machine tool manufacturing or distributing business and I walked into your office one day and told you I could supply you with a list of names and addresses of people who have already shown an interest in buying your machine tools, what would you say?

I'll bet your first question would be 'How much?'

'£100 per name and address,' I'd reply. And I'd stand a good chance of getting thrown out on my ear.

But consider the nature of the machine tool business. You have a salesforce out there, making most of their calls on prospective customers, rather than existing customers – because machine tools is essentially a 'one-off' business, and highly competitive. You'd be up against forty or more competitors on every sales territory.

Your salesforce makes a lot of cold canvass calls. On average, for every ten cold canvass calls, the salesforce gets face-to-face with one positive prospect – a 'warm one'. But a call, any kind of call, you know costs at least £40 to make. That's a simple piece of arithmetic – total cost of the salesforce divided by the number of calls made, for any given period of time.

So one 'warm one' costs £400 if you let your salesforce handle the job. And you threw me out on my ear when I offered you a list of warm ones for one-quarter the cost.

That's how people often look at the cost of exhibiting.

I used this example because recently I was involved, as a consultant, in the planning and manning of an exhibition stand at the International Machine Tool Exhibition.

The budget, not including the cost of the machines on display, was £120,000. Over the duration of the Exhibition, the stand manning staff sold all the machines on the stand and logged the names and addresses of more than 1,200 people they hitherto didn't know existed, who set foot on the stand and showed an interest in the machines.

If we assume that the sale of the actual machines on display covered the labour costs of all the staff involved on the stand, we're left with 1,200 'warm ones' and a cost of £120,000 for being there.

That's £100 per logged name and address!

Whatever your business, this is the way you should cost out the viability of the exhibitions in which you consider participating.

Usually, exhibitions fall into two categories:

(a) Major trade events at which the company has been exhibiting for years – the ones which it must attend if it wishes to be taken seriously.

(b) New exhibitions, either a new venture for the company or newly developed events which cover emerging markets where your company is developing new products or services.

If you get stuck with the task of organising your company's stand at an exhibition, you'll find it's one of the most time-consuming and nerve-wracking jobs you'll ever have to do in your entire career. However, if you do it well, you will have learnt a lot about project management and about working with colleagues (over whom you have no line authority) to make things happen.

An exhibition is 'live', and, like all live events, you gotta get it right first time.

If you don't get it right – you've got it wrong. There are no instant replays at a live event.

Getting it *right first time* means bringing every element of the exhibition – product placement, set construction, computer graphics, technical equipment, personnel, you name it – together at the same time. All working smoothly. Everything has to be of the highest quality and closely supervised. There are no shortcuts.

Given all this, the best way to handle organising an exhibition is to turn it into **a project**.

There is plenty of literature around about project management. Read some of it – you're going to need it. There are also lots of inexpensive software packages which you can download into your computer and which will be invaluable in helping you manage the project.

About sixty separate events go into planning an exhibition – and about another dozen that are essential after the event.

The first thing to decide in planning the project is to decide what you want from the exhibition. What's the aim and objective of the project. Presumably, one of your aims is to be different – to differentiate both your stand and your products from those of your competitors, who will be exhibiting around you. You will want to attract new customers and re-establish relationships with existing ones. All the specific reasons for the exhibition must be answered and understood before you start the project. But your number one aim and objective will be to make sales.

A project (in this context) is usually an undertaking which is outside the mainstream activities of the company's departments, organised and supervised by personnel from those departments reporting to a project head who is not their line manager.

Think about it. Given the above definition, the chances for things going wrong, for feathers being ruffled, for Chinese whispers and bad communications, are legion. So, if you are in charge, learn the rules of project management and apply them rigidly. Simplified, they are as follows:

1 **Agree objectives**

2 **Establish the chain of command**. If you're in charge it must be understood by everybody else that you carry the full authority to make the project successful.

3 **Establish individual responsibilities**. Ensure everyone knows their role.

4 **Plan everything *back* from D-day – Exhibition Opening Day**. This is where the computer software is useful – critical dates can be established on time charts. Plan critical dates to allow sufficient time to avoid any last minute panic.

5 **Every one involved in the project must have access to project details** and time charts which means allowing access to the computer program. Everybody must understand key dates.

6 **Meetings**. Have regular meetings but they must be attended by everyone. Arrange them well in advance.

7 **All information must be circulated** without fail – minutes of the meetings, details of actions, information on changes.

8 **Progress must be chased relentlessly**. If you can, appoint a progress chaser –possibly a secretary. Get her to update the computer program and the chart.

9 **Watch the budget**. Check it regularly. Allow a percentage in the budget for unforeseen occurrences.

10 **Resist alterations**. Once key events and dates are agreed, resist any changes or other alterations.

If possible, appoint a firm of well-qualified exhibition stand organisers. Check around to make sure they have a good reputation. These people don't come cheap but they can save you a lot of time and trouble and, if you make them understand your requirements exactly, they will do a good job.

However, you will still have to treat the event as a project, the difference being that you will be dealing with a group of outsiders who will accept your authority more readily and who have a wealth of experience in event organising. They can see the pitfalls.

If you can't appoint exhibition stand organisers and the whole project is down to you, make sure your stand contractors are well-qualified.

On the day before the exhibition, meet with your team and/or the exhibition stand organisers to double-check everything – the stand, the furniture, the equipment, services, security.

Check that everything needed is on the stand, in its right place and in good working order and condition. Check that the mobile telephones all work – and the fax and modem for internet connection. Ensure everybody knows the stand telephone numbers. Advise the people actually manning the stand of their hours. Allow two hour shifts – two hours on, one hour off. Organise off-duty manning staff to collect competitive literature.

Finally, make sure there is a proper system for logging inquiries and collect everyone's enquiries twice each day. If THEY get stolen, you get fired!

THE CRUNCH

'Our stand at a trade exhibition gives us an opportunity to get at our competitors' customers But it also gives our competitors an opportunity to get to our customers.

So this is a game we simply must be best at, or we shouldn't do it at all.'

Expense Accounts

The only time your salespeople aren't actually costing you money in expenses, is when they are standing in front of a customer. At all other times, their meters are running.

Whether they're driving the company car, calling you on the company mobile, using the company laptop or desktop computer at home – even when they're sleeping in the hotel bedroom paid for by the company – they're costing money.

Salespeople's expenses typically run between a quarter and a third of their total costs. What's more, they're pretty well fixed; there may be slight variations depending upon total sales volume and/or number of orders taken, but not enough to make any difference. So, the considerable cost of expenses must be factored in when you are contemplating recruiting extra salespeople.

Keep a watchful eye on expenses, but don't make a big issue of them unless you suspect someone of cheating. Let your sales force know that, once a month, you take one person's expenses, at random, and check everything thoroughly. Even better, have your secretary (who almost certainly has a better eye for detail than you) check two or three expense forms each month.

Mature salespeople know what they need to spend to get the job done and they do spend. They don't cheat and they keep good records. Tell your sales team that that is the standard you expect and you'll probably get it.

Make sure the expenses claim form used by your salespeople is designed to give you the kind of detailed information for which you need to search. Also have the claim form separate out VAT. You'll be your company accountant's friend for life.

There follows an example of a well-designed monthly expenses claim form.

NAME			PETROL AND OIL		REPAIRS		HOTELS		MEALS		FARES		PHONE		CUSTOMER ENTERTAINMENT			OTHER EXPENSES			GRAND TOTAL	
															CUSTOMER'S NAME	£	P	DETAILS	£	P	£	P
DAY	DATE	JOURNEY	£	P	£	P	£	P	£	P	£	P	£	P								
MON																						
TUE																						
WED																						
THU																						
FRI																						
MON																						
TUE																						
WED																						
THU																						
FRI																						
MON																						
TUE																						
WED																						
THU																						
FRI																						
MON																						
TUE																						
WED																						
THU																						
FRI																						
MON																						
TUE																						
WED																						
THU																						
FRI																						

DATE

TOTALS
Less Private Mileage
Total Business Petrol

Less Private Petrol
TOTAL CLAIMED

HQ USE ONLY
TAX EXCLUSIVE VALUES

79

F

Field Training

Field training, or 'on-the-job training' is an essential part of the training and development of salespeople. However, many sales managers avoid spending regular time making calls in the field with each of their salespeople. They say it's because they're too busy. Which is a pretty lame excuse bearing in mind that training, both on and off the job, is one of the primary tasks of sales managers.

The real reason is because there are no clear-cut objectives for the day's training, which creates a feeling of embarrassment between the manager and the salesperson. Also, the salesperson is pretty convinced that the manager is checking up. Which of course, to a certain extent, the sales manager is. Or at least, checking up on the salesperson's performance. But, as with everything, there is a right way and a wrong way to go about training in the field.

Field training should be a carefully planned process in which the salesperson learns by doing. The manager should take on the role of the salesperson's mentor, or even better, the 'coach'.

A coach knows the game. He or she watches a trainee's performance closely and evaluates it, picking up those areas which the trainee needs to work on to improve. The coach isn't there to criticise, the coach is there to help the trainee WIN.

If salespeople understand the role of field training as being akin to that of a sports coach, they will come to accept and even welcome it.

To make field training more effective, the sales manager should:

1 Set pre-call objectives with the salesperson. Practice the sales presentation. Agree what is to be accomplished. Identify the objectives. Secure the sale.

2 Make the call with the salesperson as a *non-participating observer.*

3 After the call, contribute positive reinforcement as well as constructive and helpful critiques of performance.

4 Conduct the after sale analysis (the kerb-side conference), by letting the salesperson do most of the talking.

The following is an example of a kerbside conference, with manager and salesperson contributing to an analysis of one sales call:

Kerbside Conference
Example Dialogue
(M = Manager, S = Salesperson)

Notes

M Well, how do you think it went? — *Immediate involvement by questioning.*

S Pretty well. I got the order, didn't I?

M Yes, well done. That's the major objective, of course. But do you think it was the right order? — *Sincere praise. Manager beginning to probe.*

S Well, I don't think he could have taken any more stock of the product. He doesn't have the space.

M What about our other products? — *Manager exposing limitations of call objective.*

(contd. overleaf)

S I suppose I could have introduced one or two of the new quality lines. But the opportunity didn't arise.

M Is there anything that could have been done to create an opening?

Showing that call could have been better prepared.

S Quite honestly I was so pleased with the order that I forgot about anything else.

Salesperson admits that once he got the order he did not continue (very common mistake).

M Perhaps if you had planned the call better, might you have built in a mention?

Manager is still questioning – identified call planning weakness.

S I suppose so. But in any case as you heard, the buyer says he has no space for any more products.

M Yes, what about that objection? Did you believe he meant that?

Manager is now probing second weakness.

S His shelves certainly looked full.

Salesperson beginning to get defensive.

M But won't he have to stock somebody's quality line. Our research as you know shows that the market is trending that way; 20% of the customers are now in this segment, aren't they?

Manager is identifying possible objection answer.

S Yes, I should have mentioned it. I guess what he really meant was that he's happy with his current supplier of that type of product.

Salesperson is shifting around.

M Would you not have uncovered his real reason if you had pressed a little harder there?

S I've never been very good at that kind of thing. It can only lead to an argument.

Salesperson very defensive. This is the third attempt to justify his failure to press the buyer.

M Not necessarily. Anyway we can come back to that later. Overall how would you summarise that interview?

Manager is at fault. Should have gently pursued until gained acceptance. He will now have to tell the salesperson of the deficiency.

S Well, on the good side, I got an order but I suppose with a bit better planning I could have got some of the new products in. But I don't know how if the man simply didn't have the space.

More balanced view than originally from salesperson.

Recognises his planning failure but still defensive over the space objection.

M Well, let's take those two points of preparation and objection handling. First the basic aim of preparation is to ensure we have specific objectives for each call. This avoids the danger that the call might simply be a rambling conversation. From these defined targets which are derived from a study of the customer record card we can structure the whole interview – how to open, what objections are likely and how to close. You probably remember we spent a lot of time on this on the initial training programme?

Manager now instructs.

S Yes, now you remind me -it's called structuring, isn't it?

Salesperson is beginning to remember.

M That's right. It makes sure we don't overlook opportunities simply because we've got an order for something. It also helps particularly in predicting objections. Knowing this buyer and knowing you wished to

(contd. overleaf)

introduce new lines, could you not have forecast that he would object that he had no space?

Back to the space objection. Manager is still having to gain acceptance

S Yes, I suppose so. He's always moaning that he hasn't got enough room. And he gets upset if you push him.

Salesperson is still defensive

M Quite understandably. You must agree with him that his space is limited but you could have brought the research with you and shown him how the market is changing. Perhaps he would have realised then that he cannot afford to overlook this important group of customers. Also as the research was done by an independent agency, it is not you that he has to argue with. Remember – we called this the Third Party Reference or Testimonial technique?

Manager is instructing now. His points are perfectly valid but could lose impact because of the failure to really identify the nature of the salesperson's lack of skill.

S That's right. But I didn't have the survey with me. I don't really understand this research business, you know. The boys and I have often said it baffles us.

At last the salesperson admits that he/she does not really understand the research.

M Right, we will discuss the use of research surveys at the next sales meeting. But before that meeting, which is a week on Tuesday, I want you to read the latest survey and make sure you always have it with you. It contains many good sales points. Also I want you to re-read the training notes on preparation and objection handling techniques. In fact, it

Manager specifies action and time periods.

Note linking of field training to sales meetings as research problem probably common in sales force.

Manager should also note for possible inclusion in initial training. Self-training specified and linked to action. Delegation but with

handling techniques. In fact, it would be valuable if you could give a session at the meeting after next on 'How I plan my calls'. Pop in next time you are in the office and we will discuss it in more detail.

Now for the next call, let's start practising some preparation. Get out your record card and let's see if we can set some specific goals. You did very well to get an order at all. You can do even better next time and get a bigger one.

accountability. Training continues on call preparation, probably to be followed by rehearsal and role-playing of handling space objection.

Final words of encouragement.

The sales manager should be careful not to participate in the selling action. Observation is essential and the sale should not become a two-on-one performance, where the objective of getting the order becomes more important than the objective of training the salesperson.

The sales manager is supposed to be a coach – not a player – and should stay out of the game no matter what the score. If the sales manager jumps into the sale and says in effect, 'let me take it from here', the salesperson knows that the training has stopped. Whatever the reason for the sales manager's jumping in, it will be interpreted as inherently critical. The sales manager is no longer the coach. Don't do it unless you and the salesperson have agreed a basis of signalling in advance of the calls. Examples of this might be:

(a) If the salesperson scratches the left ear in a particular way, this signal means 'I know I will appear to you to have lost it, but actually I know what I am doing. Please keep quiet.'

(b) If the salesperson rubs the side of the nose in a particular way, this signal means 'I've lost it. Jump in quick and bale me out.'

Finding New Customers

Every salesperson should be continuously on the lookout for new business, for without new business, your company cannot grow. And if it's not going forward – it must be going backwards.

Almost always, salespeople tend to concentrate the majority of their time on known customers – those who have bought before. They neglect (or sometimes deliberately avoid) breaking new ground. The reasons for this range from lack of confidence to fear of being turned away, or even laziness.

Salespeople often feel that breaking new ground is much more difficult than it is, and far more difficult than selling repeat business. This is because they don't really understand how to do it – or why it is so essential.

The Five Basic Rules of Finding New Customers

1   Every business loses customers and must find new ones to replace the ones lost – this is a fact of life that every company has to live with. The trick is to find sufficient new customers to provide an even greater volume of sales than would have come from those customers who are lost.

2   Finding new customers is one of the salesperson's prime functions. It can also be one of the most enjoyable and satisfying functions as well.

3   All salespeople should know how many new customers they need to find to make their new business targets.

4   New customers must be sought after on a regular, continuous, systematic basis, not just on a couple of odd sunny days every month or when time allows.

5   All salespeople should know what kind of new customers they should be looking for.

How Many New Customers are Needed?

All salespeople should have an annual new business target. Let's assume in this example that it's £100,000 a year.

Divide the salesperson's average order value into the new business target. Let's assume the salesperson's average order value is £5,000 for New Business.

Therefore the salesperson needs 20 new business orders – either from one new business customer in the first year, or (more likely) one order each from 20 new business customers, to reach his or her target.

From the salesperson's personal performance record, the sales manager can establish the salesperson's new business calls to new orders performance ratio.

Let's assume it is 7:1 (seven new calls to one new order). This means that the salesperson needs to make 140 (20 x 7) new business calls in a year to secure 20 new customers. Allowing for holidays, etc. and assuming a working year of ten months, this means 14 new business calls per month.

Where to Find Them

No country on earth is as well blessed for trade directories as the UK. Counting both general and specialist directories, there are over 4,000 of them – most published annually.

Get yourself a comprehensive list. You can find such lists in the Directory of Annuals and Guides, published by British Rate and Data or in Current British Directories, published by CBC Research Ltd.

Some examples of useful general directories are:–

- UK Kompass
- Two volumes of Sell's Directory of Products and Services
- Kellys Eight Regional Directories which cover the UK by town and county. and which list 95,000 companies.

Also, check the situations vacant pages in local newspapers. When companies require new staff you should assume it means they are expanding, which usually indicates there are prospects for new business.

Referrals (otherwise known as Fishing)

For salespeople, fishing is a must. Make sure your salespeople fish at every opportunity. Train them well and monitor their ability in the field. Salespeople should take advantage of every opportunity to ask their customers "by the way, before I go, do you know anyone else in this area who might be interested in our ...?" It's a way of finding new customers without spending time or money. It's the best and easiest way possible, even better because existing customers can make the introductions for your sales people.

For more detail on this crucial element of the Selling process, read John Fenton's 'How to Find New Customers', part of his 'The Profession of Selling' series.

Fishing

Fishing is by far the most popular participative sport in the UK. There are over 4 million practicing fisherpeople. As a sales manager, you've got to make your salespeople expert fisherpeople.

It is the only way to find new customers without spending time or money. It is also the best way and the easiest way. It is the best way because your existing customers make introductions for you.

Draft your Referral (Fishing) script below. Try to develop at least six consecutive questions, ending with 'I wonder ... would you give one of your colleagues a ring for me, while I am here, to see if he'd have time to see me today. I've got an hour unallocated, between 3 and 4 this afternoon.'

Q1_____

Q2_____

Q3_____

Q4_____

Q5_____

Q6_____

Forecasting

Sales Forecasting is one of the most important activities in your job specification. Why? Because, the sales forecast is *the most important document in your company.*

Top management uses it to allocate resources among the company's various functions and to control the operations of the firm. Finance uses it to project cash flows, to decide on capital spending and to establish operating budgets. Production uses it to determine production quantities, schedules and control stock. Personnel uses it to plan people requirements. Purchasing uses it to plan the company's material requirements. Marketing uses it to plan marketing and sales programmes.

And, of course the sales forecast is also fundamentally important in planning and evaluating the sales effort of your people. Sales managers use it for setting targets and as a basis for salary and commission levels and in judging the effectiveness of the field sales force.

The sales forecast must always be arrived at against a background of the prevailing economic conditions in the country and also against the current and predicted growth of the market/s in which your company operates.

Failure to consider the economic background and market growth can result in the forecast being wildly inaccurate and both you and other senior management accepting a forecast that bears no relation to market conditions.

For instance, you would probably be very pleased if your forecast predicted a sales increase of 25% the following year. However that 25% wouldn't look so good if you find from your marketing department that economic conditions next year are expected to be very good, with interest rates predicted to go down, whilst the market into which you are selling is expected to increase by 30%. The sales forecast you thought was pretty good now looks pretty sick.

However, when getting your salespeople to predict the next year's sales from their territories, it's best not to get them thinking too much about prevailing market conditions, growth predictions and economic trends.

Salespeople are notoriously poor estimators, tending to be vastly over-optimistic when the economy is booming and vastly pessimistic when things are not so good. By and large, salespeople see a vested interest in forecasting on the low side – below expectations (both yours and their own).

They know their commission, bonuses, etc are likely to be based upon the figures they achieve. So, they tend to make the achievement easy and forecast pessimistically.

In the end, however, there's no doubt that the sales forecast must start with the individual salespeople. They are the only people who know, or at least have a good idea, of what sales level can be achieved in the following year. And it's the sales force that has to be committed to the task of achieving the forecast sales.

You'll never really commit a salesperson to achieving any objective if he or she hasn't been involved in deciding what the objective should be, and why.

It Takes Three Months!!!

It takes three months for field salespeople to produce a meaningful forecast of the business their territory should produce next year. Not three months solid work, of course, but three months during which the salespeople are making their normal calls, and at the same time, asking an additional question or two of everyone they meet, such as:

> "I've got to produce a forecast of what business will come from my territory next year. Could you give me any idea of what your requirements are likely to be between January and December?"

– and so on. Think of the commitment they get from the customers for next year, on this basis.

Don't expect an accurate forecast if you give your salespeople a week in which to prepare it. All you'll get is an overall guess based on last year. Totally useless.

Use a form for sales forecasting like the example opposite. Get your salespeople to complete as many forms as they can over the three month period. Get them also to list businesses in order of potential – largest first, smallest last.

You'll see that the form allows for each individual customer or prospect to be forecast according to quarterly periods and to the products/services involved. There is also a column for noting the minimum calls the salesperson reckons need to be allocated to each customer next year – another thing that can be agreed with the customer when asking those forecasting questions.

Having the 'Minimum Calls' column next to the 'Total Forecast' column isn't just an accident. You know how many calls each of your salespeople is likely to be able to make during next year. So count up the calls allocated in the 'Minimum Calls' column, from the top of the first sheet, until you arrive at the total calls possible in the year. Draw a line across the Forecast sheet at that point. Then add up the business in the 'Total Forecast' column from the top of sheet one until you get to the line. That's the total amount of business this salesperson has got time to get, if you accept the minimum call figures and current performance.

You now have a superb starting point from which to decide, by agreement, the salesperson's final sales target for next year. You have everything you need to get the very best out of every salesperson.

When you have established the sales target for each salesperson, you can total them all on a sheet like the one shown opposite and produce a total company forecast, which will be the basis for planning for production, finance, personnel and everyone else.

After all this, all you will have to do is achieve the Forecast!

LIST CUSTOMERS IN ORDER OF POTENTIAL, GREATEST FIRST — **SALES FORECAST** for year _____ Salesperson **B SIMPSON** Sheet **1** of **4**

CUSTOMER	INDUSTRY CATEGORY	M&N CALLS NEEDED IN YEAR	TOTAL FORECAST	FORECAST SPREAD				PRODUCT BREAKDOWN									
				FIRST QUARTER	SECOND QUARTER	THIRD QUARTER	FOURTH QUARTER	0	1	2	3	4	5	6	7	8	9
TOTALS BROUGHT FORWARD																	
EATON & CO	C	20	2400	600	600	600	600		1800	600							
BLOGGS & SMALL	H	20	2800	600	500	500	600					1000	600	600			600
BRT	C	20	2000	600	400	500	500		2000								
H BLAND	B	20	1600	600	500		500	1000									
B SISSON & CO	H	20	1500	500		500	500			1500							
WILSON WALTON INT	H	10	1300	800		300	300			800	500						
O K VALVES	D	20	1300	400	300	400	300		800					500			
ALLAN & RICHARDS	D	6	1200	800		200	300			1200							
G & S TUBES	D	20	1000	300	200	200	300						500	500			
TOBM & CO	C	9	1000	400	100		500		300	300				200	200		
BERRY METERS	J	9	950	300	250		400					950					
ALLSOP COMPS	D	9	950	350	200		450						550			400	
POTTERSBY & CO	G	10	950	300	200	150	300			600	350						
BREEDON SMITH	G	9	900	300	300		300	300		300			300				
ASF & CO	H	6	900	450			450					450	450				
SNIPER VALVE CO	G	7	900	400	100	100	400	500						400			
WEBSTER & BLACK	H	10	900	400	100		300	400							500		
NORMAN WELDING	B	20	800	200	200	200	300	400	400								
GALAXY ELECTRICAL	H	6	800	400	200		400						800				
REDDY CATALNES	D	6	800	400			400				800						
TOTALS CARRIED FORWARD		257	24,350	9,100	3,950	3,050	8,300	2,600	5,300	5,300	1,650	2,400	3,200	2,200	700	400	600

SALES FORECAST for year _____ Salesperson **B SIMPSON**

LIST CUSTOMERS IN ORDER OF POTENTIAL, GREATEST FIRST

INDUSTRY CATEGORY	CUSTOMER	MIN CALLS NEEDED IN YEAR	TOTAL FORECAST	FORECAST SPREAD FIRST QUARTER	SECOND QUARTER	THIRD QUARTER	FOURTH QUARTER	PRODUCT BREAKDOWN 0	1	2	3	4	5	6	7	8	9
	TOTALS BROUGHT FORWARD	728	59450	23650	12050	10150	16800	6950	13550	13400	3700	6000	10300	4650	1350	1250	1000
C	FRIEDMAN-THE LOGIC	4	400	200			200		200	100							
C	DAVIS GEARING	4	400	100	100	100	100		200	100							
B	AUTOLIFT	5	550	150	50		150				150		100				
G	NIGHTHAWKS & WILBRO	6	550	100	50	50	150						350			100	
E	SOMELE ENGINEERING	3	300	100	100		100									100	100
E	RUGBY PRECISION	4	300	150		50	150							800	100		
A	APPLEGATE & CO	6	300	100	50	50	100			100				100	100		
E	FRANCIS BERWICK	3	250	100	50	50	100	250					100		50		
C	WAKEFIELDS	4	250	150	50	50	50		100		50		50				
7	A P MOTORS	3	800	100	50	50	50		100					100			
7	GENERAL ELECTRIC	4	800	50	50	50	50				100			100			
E	NORTH & TIPPETT	2	800	100			100				100				50	50	
	TOTALS CARRIED FORWARD	776	65150	24050	12500	10500	18100	7200	14150	13600	4100	6000	10900	5450	2150	1500	1100

SALES FORECAST - EXISTING CUSTOMERS AND KNOWN PROSPECTS - YEAR _____

	SALESPERSON	MINIMUM CALLS NEEDED IN YEAR	TOTAL FORECAST	FORECAST SPREAD				PRODUCT BREAKDOWN									
				FIRST QUARTER	SECOND QUARTER	THIRD QUARTER	FOURTH QUARTER	0	1	2	3	4	5	6	7	8	9
1	B STMPSON	776	65150	24050	12500	10500	18100	7200	14150	12600	4100	6000	10900	5450	2150	1500	1100
2	R BRIGGS	764	60250	22000	12000	10000	16250	8650	15200	10500	3550	5400	5200	5000	2000	800	950
3	L SUTTON	780	49500	18000	10000	9000	12500	5500	12500	9300	2200	5000	7500	4250	1500	1200	700
4	J WINTERS	795	51250	21250	12500	10500	14000	6800	13350	10300	3750	5750	8650	6800	1800	1000	850
5	G HOPKINS	841	56000	20000	12500	10000	13500	6500	16000	10000	1350	5500	8000	5550	1300	800	800
6	A ROLFE	710	51500	19500	10500	9500	12000	5000	13150	9500	2200	4500	7500	4500	2000	1500	1650
7	B STEIN	735	57000	20250	12000	10250	14500	6450	11700	10750	2750	6000	7750	5750	3900	1300	650
8	S ARMSTRONG	732	56500	19000	12500	10000	15000	6000	14000	10500	2250	6000	7500	5500	2000	2000	750
9	J JONES	705	50000	18500	10500	9000	12000	5000	11500	11000	2800	5000	7000	4000	1850	1350	500
10	W ASQUITH	832	74500	26000	15000	12500	21000	8500	18800	16500	2500	7500	12000	6000	1550	400	1350
11																	
12																	
	TOTALS	7560	578650	208550	120000	101250	148850	65600	138650	110750	28950	56650	85000	57850	200050	11850	9300

95

G

Growth

Every company needs growth, otherwise it dies very quickly or is devoured by its competitors.

There are four ways for the average company to secure growth:

1 Increasing its share of existing markets with its existing products or services, normally at the expense of its competitors (Market Penetration).

2 Finding and developing new markets for its existing products or services (Market Development).

3 Developing new products or services which can be sold to existing markets (Product Development).

4 Diversification – usually by acquisition.

Most sales managers are concerned mainly with 1 and 2. Some take a partial interest in 3. Few get involved in 4 – that's left to the board of directors (but who makes recommendations to the board, and on what criteria do acquisitions take place?)

Growth is not achieved simply by increasing prices, nor by maintaining one's market share in an expanding market. Yet, many practicing managers fall into the trap of thinking things are going well when really the business is rapidly losing ground.

The Five Year Plan

Not long ago, I consulted for a company – well respected in its field – that had just put the finishing touches to its five-year plan.

Turnover projections were based on an objective of approximately 15% growth per year over the five years. Current turnover was £5,000,000 and the projection looked like this:

First year turnover	£ 5,000,000
Second year turnover	£ 5,750,000
Third year turnover	£ 7,050,000
Fourth year turnover	£ 8,100,000
Fifth year turnover	£ 9,300,000
Sixth year turnover	£10,700,000

A new factory extension was allowed for in the plan, to cope with future production. However, there was no provision whatever for new product development. Also, apart from plans to increase sales office secretarial staff at strategic points in line with the turnover progression, the only other consideration given to sales operation's part in this planned expansion, was to budget for the employment of one extra salesperson for every £1,000,000 increment of new turnover. The £1,000,000 figure was decided because the average turnover currently achieved by each of the existing salespeople was between £800,000 and £1,000,000 per year.

The directors of the company were happily looking forward to the next five years, well content with the projected profit margins. They saw no insurmountable problems in funding the necessary number of new salespeople and training them up to effectiveness. They saw no shortfall developing in the market potential, or holdups through any failure to win slices of business from competitors. They had even allowed for the costs of replacing some of their salespeople who might leave during the five-year period.

So when I suggested to these directors that the projected turnover could be achieved without the need to increase the size of the present sales force by even one person, you can imagine the cynical smiles.

I showed how I arrived at my suggestion. "If prices increase by 5% a year during this next five years, what increase in turnover will this give the company without another finger needing to be lifted?"

Answer –

First year	£ 5,000,000
Second year	£ 5,250,000
Third year	£ 5,512,500
Fourth year	£ 5,788,125
Fifth year	£ 6,077,530
Sixth year	£ 6,381,406

So I said, "You're a significant way toward your five year target on straight price increase alone."

My next question was, "What kind of personal development programme have you got for your salespeople?"

This question was greeted by a somewhat puzzled, "What do you mean?"

"Well," I replied, "if your salespeople are pulling in £1,000,000 worth of business this year, what scope are you going to give them to expand on this? What encouragement is there for them to attain £1,100,000 next year? What back-up to make this attainment easier? What extra rewards if they move on to £1,500,000? What on-going training to develop their knowledge of the company's products, the applications of those products and the markets for these applications?"

"If your salespeople continue to pull in just £800,000 to £1,000,000 worth of business a year," I continued, "how long will it be before they get fed up, lose that all-important job satisfaction, reckon they're in a rut and not getting anywhere – and quit?"

The puzzled frowns gradually turned to genuine surprise. I rubbed salt into the wound.

"To lose a good salesperson and have to replace him or her at short notice would cost the company several months new business turnover, the loss of a fair slice of goodwill, plus about £40,000 to train the new salesperson up to full effectiveness. Even then, there would be some uncertainty – whether or not the new salesperson will make the grade, and the cost of having to start all over again if he or she fails to make it."

Surprise was changing to a certain amount of apprehension.

"Wouldn't it be much more sensible to have a planned personal

98

development programme for each salesperson. Then each person can develop his or her knowledge, abilities, territory, customers, sense of importance, his or her rewards based upon their own achievements – all this giving them the job satisfaction and pride that will keep them working effectively for you for many years to come?"

Nods and raised eyebrows.

"Suppose, for example, each salesperson could increase his or her turnover by 10% per year, in true terms, excluding price increases. And suppose they were to be rewarded accordingly – in addition to their usual salary increases linked to the cost of living index – do you think this would provide them with some significant job satisfaction?"

Emphatic affirmatives.

"So how does this 10% personal improvement target linked to your calculated 5% price increases per year, influence your five year turnover projection?"

The answer of course, is obvious. The company could reach its £10.7 million target with no additional salespeople, and with much less risk of losing the salespeople it already employed.

Profits significantly increased. Problems significantly reduced.

The five-year plan was amended forthwith. But it wouldn't have been fair to leave those directors with their revised five-year plan, just at that stage. So a few more questions were submitted.

Will the Salespeople do it on their own?

"Would you have confidence in your present sales force achieving a 10% per year increase in true turnover on their own – without supervision, without encouragement, without help, or without you at least monitoring the results as they happen?"

Heavy sighs. Comments like, "Thought it would be too good to be true."

"So, how are you going to make sure it all happens? How are you going to monitor and measure your salespeople's performance as the months and the years go by, to make sure the desired improvement is achieved? How are you going to establish what back-up is necessary, in what area of the country, or in what sector of the market or section of the product range? How are you going to calculate the amount of advertising and mail shots required in each territory, to generate the kind of response each salesperson needs in order to make his 'new business' target attainable without tears or frustration, or weeks of door-knocking? How are you going to make sure each salesperson does the selling part of his job as effectively as possible, and the planning part of his job as efficiently as possible? How are you going to pinpoint problems in any salesperson's effectiveness, quickly – so that you can rectify the problems just as quickly and stay on target? How are you going to get the salespeople to monitor their territories so that they keep you fully aware of how the market is doing so you don't miss out on any potential business?"

Hands in the air.

"Stop, stop! We haven't the time to do all that. Our sales manager can't even spare the time to get out in the field with the salespeople more than once or twice a month. He's already inundated with more paperwork than he can handle."

"But does the paperwork they handle at present give them all the information I've just mentioned? And in a form that makes it easy to use? If their reporting and control systems are really working, it shouldn't need to take more than one hour a week of their time. My guess is that most of the paperwork with which they get loaded at present isn't really necessary, or doesn't really do the job it was intended to do.

"Most sales forces won't achieve any meaningful improvement in performance on their own. In fact, the reverse is true. Left to their own devices, most salespeople will gradually decline in performance. Every sales force needs a strong, determined, dedicated, enthusiastic sales manager. A leader. A manager who really manages. Someone who can achieve results through the efforts of other people – his team. Not a promoted salesperson who still thinks of him or herself as a salesperson.

"And that sales manager, that team leader, must have at his or her fingertips all the information, figures, ratios and statistics which will enable them to plan their next move, and the shape of the improvement target for each individual salesperson in his team."

"What kind of information?" the directors demanded.

"How many days a year are available to the sales force for actual selling? How many face-to-face calls can they make? Which existing customers are worth calling on in the next year – and why: which ones are not worth calling on – and why not? How much business will each of these existing customers produce next year? How many calls will the sales force need to make to secure this repeat business? How much time does the sales force have available to seek new business? What proportion of the total business comes from quotations? What is the conversion ratio of quotations into orders? What is the average order value for (a) repeat business and (b) new business?

"How many quotations must be generated to get to target? What is each salesperson's average miles per call ratio? How many of each salesperson's calls are made by appointment?"

After an hour's discussion and quite a few internal telephone calls, the directors had to admit that their company could make a reasonable guess at only four of these twelve questions. But only a guess. No one was actually recording any data from which precise figures could be derived. This appeared to worry them.

"You have a significant element of 'Fudge Factor' in your sales operation", I said.

"Fudge Factor?" the directors chorused. "Fudge Factor? What the hell do you mean by that?"

Fudge Factor

'Fudge Factor' is the result of management not insisting on their sales force accepting and working to the same kind of disciplines expected of production, accounts, transport and all other departments in the company.

Fudge Factor is a term coined by Philip Lund, author of *Compelling Selling and Sales Reports, Records and Systems*. Lund's words on the subject are as follows:

'I have always found it hard to understand why people who run successful businesses consistently allow themselves to be betrayed by their field sales forces. For some strange reason, these otherwise competent executives accept a level of fudge factor from their sales operation that they would not tolerate from the other departments of their business.

In sales planning, targets and performance can be quantified and controls can be exercised through numbers just as easily as they can in production or in management accounting. The problem most businesses have had in the past, however, has been to discard existing outdated sales procedures and to replace them without disruption by a complete, yet simple, system that would rationalise their sales planning and control requirements.

No sales control system can replace the function of good field sales management, of course, but with the right system, this management will undoubtedly become much more efficient.'

As with most managers struggling to see the light for the first time, a few comparisons had to be made to emphasise the fact that Fudge Factor existed, and ran rampant through their organisation.

"Let's look at Customer Records," I suggested. "Would you allow your accountant to jot down his accounts in a little black book and take them with him when he leaves your employ?

"Would you allow your production blue prints to be just casual sketches, and again taken away to another company when a draughtsman leaves?

"So what happens when one of your salespeople leaves? Do you get back from them, before they go, all their records and personal information on the customers and prospects in their territory? And if you do, are these records such that you can give them to a successor so that new salespeople can get their teeth into the job with the minimum of disruption of your sales effort?

"In fact, do you actually have a standard customer record system which you provide for your salespeople, or do you expect each salesperson to devise and operate their own system?"

The silence was deafening.

"Let's look at Forward Planning," I continued. "Do you demand from your accounts department a financial plan that enables the company to maintain adequate cash flow?

"Do you expect production to know what they are going to produce next week?

"Do you allow your delivery vans to go where they please?

"So, do you get from your sales people a plan of where they intend to go next week? And more importantly, what they intend to do when they get there?

"Production knows its capacity, yet how many of your salespeople have worked out their order capacity for the next twelve months?

"And finally, if I may add a question on quality control – doubtless you take note of the amount of wastage of materials in your factory, and of the number of rejects and the scrap rates. Your accounts department is also keeping a close watch on all outstanding invoices, to make sure every customer pays his bills within a reasonable time. All the products in the factory are subject to strict quality control and testing. But to what extent does your sales manager measure, inspect and test the quality of his salespeople's performance?"

"Enough!" cried the directors. "What do you suggest we do?"

"Well, the first thing to do," I replied, "is to try to establish the extent to which 'fudge factor' has taken a grip on your sales organisation."

I handed each director a checklist. "Answer the eighteen questions (as listed in the ACTION TIME list), and then let's see what we can do to rectify all the 'no' answers."

Any reader who logs more than six nos on this checklist has a few major problems to solve. Read the section on Performance Improvement to find out how to start measuring all these things with the minimum of paperwork and time commitment.

	(Tick the appropriate column)	
	Yes	No
Do you provide your salespeople with a standardized method for keeping customer records?		
Do your salespeople keep their customer records up to date – and USE them?		
Do you make sure a salesperson who leaves the company doesn't take his customer records with him?		
Do you know how much prospecting work your salespeople need to do to achieve the company's 'New Business' target?		
If you can answer 'Yes' to question 4, do you know if your salespeople are actually doing the amount of prospecting work required?		
Do you receive a detailed plan from your salespeople of where they will be		
Are more than 40% of your salespeople's calls 'By Appointment'?		
Do you know how much business your salespeople are chasing that your company has quoted for?		
Do you know how much of this business is likely to result in firm orders next month?		
Do your salespeople prepare for you a forecast of how much business they reckon they will produce for the company during the next period?		
Is this forecast in a sufficiently detailed form so that you can pinpoint any specific customer that isn't coming up to expectations?		
Are the action reports you receive from your salespeople sufficiently legible, detailed and accurate for the company to produce a quotation and be certain it will fulfil the customer's requirements?		
Do your salespeople submit a weekly report of the customers they have called upon – and what happened?		
If the answer to question 13 is 'Yes', does anyone use the information on the weekly reports, rather than just file them away after a general check?		
Do you know if any salespeople are neglecting part of your product range?		
Do you know your company's average order value?		
Do you know your company's 'calls to quotations' ratio?		
Do you know your company's 'quotations to orders' ratio?		
Totals		

H

Habits

A habit is an automatic way of behaving – the emphasis being on the word 'automatic'.

The only difference between an act and a habit is repetition.

Many acts become routines. A routine is usually something we incorporate into our lives which becomes almost unnoticeable. For instance, from a young age, all of us were taught to clean our teeth first thing in the morning. That quotidian act has become a routine. We get up and clean our teeth. There are very good reasons for cleaning our teeth, but we probably rarely think about them. We're in a routine.

Getting dressed every morning is a routine. However, some people, when they get dressed, develop the habit of putting one particular shoe on before the other. There's no logical reason why they do that – they just do it. Within the routine, they have developed a habit. But as we all have to put both shoes on anyway, the habit of putting the left shoe on before the right makes absolutely no difference to our lives.

Some repeated acts become not so much routines as bad habits. Ask any smoker. A smoker starts with one cigarette. If the act is repeated a few times it becomes a habit – a bad one. (Do you know any smokers who don't want to stop?)

Alternatively, repeated acts can become good habits. If, in your job as a sales manager, you repeat the act at close of business of scheduling the major events for the following day, after a couple of weeks, you will have developed a good habit. Within months, it's a standard routine. A good one.

Sales managers can easily develop bad habits.

For instance, because they are who they are, some sales managers regularly interrupt when other members of the sales team are talking. The sales manager has a view on everything and he or she wants that view heard. Very soon this act of interrupting and overriding other people becomes a habit. If the sales manager is lucky, he or she will have this bad habit pointed out. Or, if they are monitoring their own performance, they will notice it for themselves.

Then it's a question of changing their act, of deliberately forcing themselves to shut up and listen – of forcing themselves to concentrate on what's being said and thereby learning something. After a while this repeated act has become a new habit – a good one.

One of the worst habits sales managers can develop is procrastination. Putting things off until the last minute, or worse still, permanently. Perhaps the sales manager procrastinates about accompanying sales people in the field or in returning difficult telephone calls. It only takes a few acts of procrastination for it to become a habit.

Habitual procrastination indicates some form of distorted thinking, usually based on emotional factors. Maybe it's a lack of self-belief. It's certainly a kind of motivational paralysis. The way to overcome procrastination, or other bad habits which get in the way of your effectiveness is to use *positive re-programming statements*.

Most of our negative bad habits are in our sub-conscious mind because we've 'self-talked' them so often, they've changed from acts into habits.

However, it's perfectly possible – and logical – for us to construct for ourselves positive 'self-talk'. The positive self-talk about whatever bad habits we've developed can be fed into our sub-conscious. Merely by self-talking positively enough, we can change our bad habits into good.

What's more, the repeated act of positive self-talk can, itself, be developed into a good habit.

This is the very crux of NLP (Neuro Linguistic Programming).

For example, if your specific negative is 'nothing ever happens to me – life is so boring' you could write a PRS (positive re-programming statement) which says 'I can make things happen'.

You can repeat this or write it, as if you were writing 'lines' at school, until that positive thought has become a good habit in your sub-conscious mind.

Good Starters for a PRS:

> I can ...
> I will ...
> I'm going to succeed with ...
> I'm lucky because ...
> This is for me ...
> It's easy ...
> Yes I can

A PRS should be:

> Positive
> Progressive (into the future)
> Brief
> Simple words
> On only one topic

A PRS should be repeat ... repeat ... repeated ...

> At least ten times a day
> Everyday
> For three weeks
> For guaranteed results
> One hundred times a day is much more effective

Remember, as Jim Ryan has said, *"motivation is what gets you started, but habit is what keeps you going."*

Holes (sudden)

One of the biggest problems a sales manager faces is having one of his salespeople suddenly quit without warning, leaving him with a large hole which has to be filled before customer service suffers too much.

Only the largest companies can afford to take on one or two young trainees, and be developing their potential in the sales office ready for a sudden hole to appear. Most sales managers have to draft a quick advertisement and hope for the best.

Two things you can do to reduce the problem:

1 Do some regular detective work and build up a file of personal contacts who might make good salespeople if and when the need arises. These might be salespeople working for other companies (but please, not your direct competitors) or even a few of your customers who yearn for the outdoor life and have the requisite temperament, abilities and motivation. Then just a phone call could get you the new person you need.

2 Hold regular meetings with the other department heads in your company, and try to establish a procedure for growing your own new salespeople, and fertilising them (covering their costs) through the jobs they are doing in the other departments of the company. The only factor against this, of course, is the sudden hole a person leaves in another department when he or she moves to sales. But holes in design, production, commercial, service, etc, are usually easier to fill or patch over than holes in sales.

Honk, Honk!

Lessons from Geese

1. As each goose
      flaps its wings,
            it creates an
                  'UPLIFT'
                        for the birds
                              that follow.
                                    By flying in a
                              'V' formation,
                        the whole flock
                  adds 71 percent
            EXTRA
      flying range.

LESSON: *People who share a sense of COMMUNITY can HELP
each other get where they are going MORE easily,
because they are travelling on the TRUST of one another.*

2. When a goose falls out of formation
   it suddenly feels the DRAG and
   RESISTANCE of flying . . . . alone.
   It quickly moves back to take
   ADVANTAGE of the lifting POWER
   of the birds in front.

LESSON: *If we have as much SENSE as geese we would stay in
formation with those HEADED where we want to go. We
should be willing to accept their HELP and to GIVE our
help to others...*

3. When the lead goose tires, it drops back into the formation and ANOTHER goose takes over the point position.

LESSON: *It pays to TAKE TURNS doing the hard tasks. We should RESPECT and PROTECT each other's unique arrangement of SKILLS, capabilities, talents and RESOURCES.*

4. The geese flying in formation HONK to encourage those up front to keep up with their speed.

LESSON: *We need to make sure honking is ENCOURAGING. In groups where there is encouragement, PRODUCTION is much greater. Individual empowerment results from QUALITY honking.*

5. When a goose gets sick, two geese drop out of formation and follow it down to HELP and PROTECT it.

LESSON: *If we have as much sense as geese we will STAND BY each other in difficult times as well as when we are STRONG.*

(With thanks to Saatchi & Saatchi)

Humour Therapy

Without humour, life would be impossible. Being happy is one of the most important ingredients of life.

For your sales team, pick naturally happy, spontaneous, enthusiastic people. They will cheer your customers up when they ring or visit them.

If your sales team is made up of miserable morons, they'll make your customers miserable, simply by indulging in what in Britain is now known as 'The National Sport'.

People buy from people they like, not from people they don't like – and the shortest route to being liked is being happy and spreading happiness – rather than gloom and despondency.

The more far-sighted sales managers have a *laughter room* – somewhere where staff can go to have a really good *laugh*. Why? Branko Bokun's serious medical book, *'Humour Therapy in Cancer, Psycho-somatic Diseases, Mental Disorders, Crime, Interpersonal and Sexual Relationships'*, spells it out:

> 'Humour heals. Chuckles cheer. Smiling soothes. Laughter is one of the best medicines of all for business stress, for worry, for strokes and heart disease.'

According to another humour-therapy expert, French doctor, Pierre Vachet:

> *'Laughter can deepen breathing, expand blood vessels, improve circulation, speed tissue healing and stabilise many body functions. But – unlike many drugs – laughter has absolutely no side effects'.*

Humour therapy is the key to why the people who laugh the most are also the most positive, the most successful and also live the longest. Strong medicine!!

Many new sales managers take themselves too seriously. Life is tough. There are new skills to learn, a sales force to manage, sales targets to meet. It's important for new sales managers to learn not to take themselves too seriously and to maintain their sense of humour.

Part of the problem is that everything in the job is new. Everything is surrounded by an enormous sense of urgency and every event looms large in the sales manager's life. However, it's important to get things into perspective. If you're sure in your own mind that you're on the right track, then relax.

Even if you've had a bad day and everything has gone pear-shaped, try to remember that in a hundred years time it won't make a whit of difference. So, develop a sense of humour.

Part of having a good sense of humour comes from having a good memory for humourous incidents and anecdotes and an appreciation of what's appropriate to the current moment. People with a good sense of humour are able to reach back into their memories and find that humorous line, joke, anecdote, whatever is appropriate to the situation at hand – and recount it.

The appropriate word, joke or recollection can relieve an awful lot of tension.

Whatever type of humour you develop, never, never be sarcastic.

Many people confuse sarcasm with humour or wit. But, if you're sarcastic, people will put you down as a cynic. Cynicism is not a trait you want to develop. Most sarcasm is funny only at someone else's expense. Sales managers who are sarcastic with their colleagues or members of their sales force quickly get themselves a reputation as a bully – one filled with bitterness and spite. Do you really want that kind of reputation?

So, keep your eyes open for those odd, quirky, warmly human and laughable situations that are bound to occur. Train your eyes to see them and, when you do, laugh at them and encourage other people to laugh at them too.

It won't get in the way of your performance. In fact, it will enhance it.

If you've got a guy
who's good in a crisis,
get rid of him
or you'll always have one.

I

Incentive Schemes

Incentives are an *external* factor. They are usually linked to Motivation (of which more later). However, motivation is an *internal* factor. Incentives can encourage motivation but always remember that *real* motivation is an attitude of mind which is fundamentally related to perception and self-discipline. It is encouraged by outside factors but not *created* by them.

Incentives can be positive external influences which encourage and improve performance. But, bear in mind that the effects of any incentive cease immediately those positive influences are withdrawn. Thus a salary, even a very high salary, is only an incentive whilst a sales person is striving for it. As soon as they've achieved the high salary (when they find their standard of living has gone up and their overdraft is bigger than ever) the salary is no longer an incentive. It has become a hygiene factor (see the notes on Frederick Hertzberg on page 155).

The primary form of incentive for sales people is commission. Commission should motivate them to a high level of selling effort and encourage sales success.

Of course, there are other, one-off incentive payments which can be paid in order to direct salespeople's efforts towards a strategic, one-time objective.

Incentives can also provide additional rewards for top performers.

Incentives can take the shape of sales contests and non-cash prizes which can be directed towards short-term, specific objectives such as selling a particular product line.

Incentives can be paid to the team as a whole but this is often a disincentive to many in the team. Much more effective are incentives paid to individuals on the basis of individual performance.

There are some basic rules about incentive schemes:

(a) They must be specific and measurable by everybody.

(b) They should be very simple, so that everybody understands how they work.

(c) Incentive schemes should be fair and equitable to all members of the sales team. And short-term. Monthly, not yearly.

(d) Scales and level of rewards should relate to the specific potential of territories or accounts.

(e) Incentive schemes should be simple and easy to administer. Something that can be worked out by your secretary and checked by you.

(f) Commission should be paid quickly after the event or sales period. However, as some sales may not ultimately materialise or may become bad debts, it is perfectly okay for two thirds of due commission to be paid on a monthly basis with the balance being accumulated to form a lump sum at the end of a quarter or half year. Any over-payments can be deducted from the balance.

(g) If these accumulated lump sums are paid just before the summer holidays and Christmas they make an even better incentive and are greatly appreciated by the sales force.

(h) Commission should never be paid on all sales achieved. If it is, there is no longer any real incentive. Commission becomes another part of the basic salary.

Commission should start when something like 75-80% of the sales target has been achieved. After that the rate should increase progressively as sales turnover increases. For example:

1% commission on target achievement of 80% and up to 100%
2% from 100% to 125% of target
3% from 125 to 150% of target
and, perhaps, 5% on any sales over 150% of target.

However, if you have many salespeople over the 150% of target, look again at their sales forecasting. They may be deliberately depressing their annual sales forecast in order to gain commission.

Don't fall for it.

Incoming Information – How to Handle It

As a newly appointed sales manager, you will be inundated with information – letters, quotations, memos, faxes, countless e-mails, phone messages on your answering machine or voice mail. You can't get away from information. Even in your car – even in your bath – the ubiquitous mobile phone will be there and someone will be calling to tell you something.

Information pouring in = information overload.

There's only way to handle this plethora of voice and print information – *ruthlessly*.

Operate the CRAFT principle

C – Consider it.

If you receive a lot of printed information – long reports, memos, letters and so on, learn to speed-read so you can get through it quickly whilst picking up the salient points.

Every piece of information you receive should be considered. But do it quickly.

If the memo, letter or whatever, needs detailed consideration, read it once then put it into the daily 'bring-up file' your secretary brings to you every day. Put the date on it for the next consideration. In the meantime, let your subconscious go to work on what needs to be done.

By the time your secretary brings it up in the file, your subconscious will have made a start on handling, solving or processing the problem.

R – Refer it.

Much information is misdirected. It comes to you when it should have gone to a colleague, direct to one of your sales people or your boss. (It's amazing how many people send out unnecessary information to the wrong people. It makes them feel as if they are doing their jobs).

Move it on quickly. Don't attach a memo to it. Handwrite whatever you've got to say on the subject onto the original piece of paper and pass it on.

Don't take a photocopy of it.

Never photocopy anything, ever, unless it's absolutely, one hundred percent necessary.

A – Act on it.

Do it. Do it now. Try to handle the paper once and only once.

F – File it.

Only in exceptional circumstances and only for the absolutely most important pieces of information. Keep your filing cabinets to the minimum. Don't forget, there are probably at least five or six copies of the particular piece of paper floating around the building. The people who've got them – the people who don't know about CRAFT – will file them. You don't need to bother.

If you ever really need the piece of paper again (unheard of – happens about one in a million times) you can get it from one of the others. Why clutter up your office with pieces of paper you're never going to look at again?

T – Throw it away.

Best solution for well over half the information you are likely to receive. Consider it, then file it in the wastepaper basket.

Information Technology

The world is now full of high-tech IT and as every month goes by, we get more and more information about newer and faster ways of transmitting information.

Undoubtedly, there is an information explosion and sales managers need to understand what new systems and technologies are available and how useful – or not – they are.

Computers are at the centre of this new technology. They provide us with the means of creating and moving information at speeds and quantities that were completely unthinkable 20 years ago.

But this explosion of technology comes at a price. Not so much the cost of the equipment, which is reducing constantly, but in the time it costs in keeping up to date with what's available, assessing how useful it is and learning how to use it.

The technology ranges from desk-top and laptop computers, to mobile phones which, linked to laptops, can thus transmit e-mail and faxes to salespeople on the road. There are floppy discs, CD-ROMs, audio conferencing, video conferencing, computer conferencing, e-mail and the world wide web.

Each of these technologies and concepts (and the many others not mentioned) can be enormously useful, or, can be a real drain on time and resources.

For instance, e-mail. Although e-mail is a great idea, much of its current use seems to be in transferring the unnecessary four times quicker. A lot of e-mail in business is dedicated to sending jokes (admittedly, very funny but often in doubtful taste) around the world.

Many sales managers find thirty or forty e-mails sitting in their in-box every morning, all asking questions or posing problems which, in the absence of e-mail, would have been answered or solved by the senders without recourse to anyone else. The British Empire, the greatest empire ever known, was run pretty efficiently by people whose 'information highway' was so slow it took three months to deliver a letter. Think about it!

Similarly, with the internet. This allows access to the world wide web and all the reference resources available within it. It too has its downside. Stories are legion of people in offices who do nothing with their time but surf the web. This may seem irrelevant to salespeople. But if they have a company computer with a modem, are they preparing quotations for customers or logging onto www.dirty stories.com?

On the other hand, some of the advances in high-tech audio visual aids need to be looked at very carefully. These days, charts and graphs stored on your laptop can be shown on a large screen at a sales conference with the use of a small, desktop projector. This is a really useful advance. It means you don't have to prepare charts and graphs and then reproduce them onto slides or acetates.(But the desktop projector costs you £4,000 to buy or £250 a day to rent!)

Also, the advances in computer-generated graphics used at large sales conferences and exhibitions are, although expensive, truly fabulous. They can make a major difference in the impact of a presentation.

And of course, salespeople using a company laptop can demonstrate visuals, concepts, designs and diagrams on the screen which, in the old days, would have been more difficult to show to customers. A laptop can be a great sales aid.

IT is an exploding world – one in which the sales manager must stay abreast of innovation.

But, use your judgement in assessing each new piece of technological wizardry. Ask yourself, is it really useful? Or is it just an attractive hi-tech toy which will merely accomplish the unnecessary fifty times faster?

THE PAPERLESS OFFICE
IS A
MYTH

J

Job Specifications and Job Descriptions

Would you believe that the majority of people in selling and sales management don't have either?

A job description is like a compass – it points you in the right direction and keeps you there. Try steering a ship without a compass.

Any sales manager without a job description should at once set about writing his own, then submit it to the powers that be for approval, or modification and then approval.

A sales manager taking on new salesmen begins with a job specification – a negotiating document used to make sure the applicant fits all the key tasks required of him – or most of them. Once taken on, this job specification is redrafted to include the specific detail on individual performance standards expected and then becomes that individual applicant's job description.

If a sales manager has to draft job descriptions from scratch for an existing sales force, the best method is to get every salesperson to draft his own, then pool the results and have the sales manager only develop the final format and the individual detailed contents for each salesperson (remember the camel which was a horse designed by a committee).

Sample Job Specification/Description
for a Salesperson

Job title: Sales engineer

Responsible to: UK sales manager

Sales area: The sales area known as area Number 5, comprising the counties of Kent, Sussex and Surrey.

Purpose: To maintain and develop business with existing customers in the area and to develop business by locating and selling to new outlets in the area.

Prime Duties and Responsibilities:

1. To acquire a thorough working knowledge of all the company's products and a thorough understanding of all their applications. To keep this knowledge up to date through regular sales meetings and product training sessions held monthly at HQ.

   Performance will be considered satisfactory when full selling proposals, including detailed financial justification, can be drafted for all customer applications to be found in area Number 5.

2. To acquire and develop all necessary professional selling skills through the meetings and training sessions referred to in (1), through attendance at outside sales training courses in accordance with the company's personal development programmes and by discussion, reading, and constant practice.

   Performance will be considered satisfactory when all eight personal performance ratios are consistently better than the company norms for these ratios, and all factors on the monthly personal selling standards record are consistently marked 'above standard'.

3. To plan the coverage of the area in the most effective and economic manner.

   Performance will be considered satisfactory when:

   (a) all customer and prospective customer records are up to date and contain full information on names, initials and positions of all contacts, best day and time to call on each contact, name of secretary, and contain a properly reported call record which specifies in all cases the aim of the next call and the firm date of the next call.

(b)   these customer and prospective customer records can be used to produce a forecast of future business expected from the area which is subsequently proved accurate.

(c)   a cycle-of-calling plan is in existence for the area and is being worked in a systematic manner.

(d)   a list of live new business prospects is being properly researched every month, prior to calling, the number of prospects on each monthly list being consistent with the known requirement for that time which has been calculated from the personal performance ratios.

(e)   at all times there is an adequate list of prospects in negotiation and that steady movement towards conclusion can be demonstrated.

(f)   a fully detailed call plan, itemising all calls to be made during the following week and with at least 60 per cent of these calls having firm appointments, is received every Friday by the UK sales manager.

4.   To report coherently and with speed and economy of words on day-to-day activities, customer installations, prevailing or changing business trends, customer complaints and satisfaction and competitors' activity, such reporting to be in accordance with directives issued from time to time by the UK sales manager and on the appropriate forms supplied for these purposes.

5.   Attendance at all regional sales meetings, national sales meetings and company-organised training sessions is mandatory.

6.   To liaise whenever necessary with the sales office manager, chief draughtsman, development manager, production manager and chief accountant to ensure a proper level of customer service and customer advice is maintained.

7.   To develop relationships with customers that further the goodwill attaching to the company name.

Performance in this respect will be considered satisfactory when sales demonstrations to prospects take place at existing customers' premises in the area on a regular basis and the reception given to company personnel when visiting customers in the area is seen generally to reflect this goodwill.

8.   The prime objective will be met when sales in the area by total, rate and product mix equate with the forecasts prepared for and the targets set for the area.

Sample Job Description
ɔnal Sales Manager or Sales Director

National Sales Manager (or Sales Director)

Managing Director (or Marketing Director)

Mai... **nsibilities:** The attainment of national sales objectives through the effective operation of the field force.

Key Tasks:

A – Attaining Sales Objectives:

The National Sales Manager will organise, lead, train, motivate and control the sales force in such a manner as to ensure the on-time attainment of sales objectives, and in particular, the attainment of:

- (a) sales targets by product
- (b) sales targets by territory
- (c) sales targets by key customers
- (d) sales activity by region
- (e) sales activity by territory

Standards of performance relative to the above are met when:

- (a) the national annual sales target is attained
- (b) the number of sales executives not attaining target is below 20% of the field force
- (c) more than 75% of the key accounts have attained or surpassed their agreed target figures
- (d) the national average effective call rate is 8 per day per sales executive
- (e) the inquiry to effective call ratio is less than 1 to 7 and is seen to be reducing
- (f) the number of product demonstrations average at least 3 per day per sales executive
- (g) the number of 'orders on the spot' averages at least 5 per week per sales executive and increasing
- (h) effective call to order ratio is less than 1 to 8 and reducing
- (i) the call to inquiry ratio is less than 1 to 1.5
- (j) the average value of orders is £750 and increasing
- (k) the number of calls made on new prospects average at least 5 per week per sales executive

124

(l)   the number of calls made on dormant customers averages at least 2 per week per sales executive

(m) the cost per call is less than £30

(n)   the average gross margin is held to 15%

(o)   the direct sales cost is held at or below 12.5%

B – Providing Sound Sales and Management Training

The National Sales Manager will provide sound sales and management training on a continued basis, and thus ensure that the overall calibre of the field force is considerably higher than that of competitors.

Standards of performance relative to the above are met when:

(a) all new sales executives joining the company are provided with a carefully designed programme of classroom and field training covering the first six months of their employ

(b) all regional sales managers have been trained to train and, in addition, are receiving regular tuition and practice in:
  (i)   Leading
  (ii)   Motivating
  (iii)   Controlling
  (iv)   Assessing

(c) all sales executives have been thoroughly trained (initially) and are constantly practiced in:
  (i)   Territory planning
  (ii)   Planning the individual sales call
  (iii)   Opening a sales discussion
  (iv)   The art of asking open, positive and quality questions
  (v)   The art of listening
  (vi)   The ability to translate technical facts into 'buyer benefits'
  (vii)   The effective use of visual selling aids
  (viii) Overcoming objections
  (ix)   Closing sales discussions positively with definite action decisions
  (x)   Following up effectively
  (xi)   Presenting a quotation effectively
  (xii)   Selling to the larger account
  (xiii) Self-analysis
  (xiv) Self-management

(d) all sales executives are thoroughly and frequently trained in the produce and its application

(e) the sales executives can answer a series of test questions on the product and its application prepared twice annually by technical department, and when the national average pass mark is in excess of 80%

(f) the regional managers are holding regional sales meetings regularly and at least once a month, where at least 50% of the meeting time is taken up with various types of sales and product training

(g) the regional managers are spending at least four days a week working with their sales executives in the field, observing their strengths and weaknesses, counseling them, recommending, demonstrating, practicing and when every sales executive receives such a visit from his regional manager every two weeks

(h) there is an up-to-date recording system showing the degree of response to training by each sales executive and manager

C – Providing the Sales Force with Leadership

The National Sales Manager will provide the sales force with leadership of the highest quality to ensure that his/her people WANT to do the things he/she wants them to do.

Standards of performance in relation to the above are met when

(a) the sales manager is seen to set the highest standards for HIMSELF/HERSELF and for all his/her staff in the following:

(i)	Appearance
(ii)	Positivity
(iii)	Sincerity
(iv)	Integrity
(v)	Enthusiasm
(vi)	Empathy
(vii)	Practising what he or she preaches
(viii)	Responsibility
(ix)	Cost-consciousness
(x)	Optimism
(xi)	Maturity
(xii)	Creativity
(xiii)	Co-operation with others
(xiv)	Drive and energy
(xv)	Capacity for hard work
(xvi)	Problem solving
(xvii)	Salesmanship
(xviii)	Statesmanship

(xix)   Diplomacy
(xx)   Human relations
(xxi)   Recognition
(xxii) Participation

(b) his/her style of management is seen to be more democratic than autocratic

(c) he/she is seen to be a good sales person of his/her ideas to people above and below his/her level

D – Controlling the Sales Force

The National Sales Manager will control the sales force and ensure that all objectives/plans are linked to simple but effective control systems. Ensure that the controls are regularly and frequently monitored by himself/herself and/or the responsible line manager. Ensure that deviations from plan are noticed quickly, and that definite action decisions are taken by him/herself and the relevant manager to ensure that performance returns to plan in the shortest possible time and that the ultimate objective is attained.

Standards of performance in relation to the above are met when:

(a) the national and regional sales managers receive the following data on a weekly basis, produced in such a manner that the cumulative (year-to-date) attainments can easily be monitored:

  (i)   sales volume by produce group and total compared with plan
  (ii)   sales activity compared with plan
  (iii) sales costs per sales executive and per region compared with plan
  (iv)   number of customer complaints compared with type of complaint
  (v)   number of field sales visits carried out with sales executives by each regional manager
  (vi)   number of calls made per grade of account

(b) Regional sales managers are seen to be reading the control data meaning fully and as soon as they receive it

(c) Regional managers are seen to be taking positive action decisions on the basis of the situation indicated by the control data

(d) The regional managers have such a thorough and dedicated understanding of the need to be constantly and dynamically working to increase averages and decrease ratios, that they are nearly always taking the right decisions before the national sales manager initiates a discussion to ask: 'What is being done?'

127

(e) There is an effective system in use to frequently and regularly monitor the results being attained in each of the company's 'blue chip' accounts and when that same system highlights such weaknesses as:

    (i)   Infrequent calling

    (ii)   Calling at too low a level

    (iii)   Talking to the wrong people

    (iv)   Talking to one person only at each time of calling

    (v)   Failure to sell through the range

    (vi)   Failure to report on the activities of competitors within the account

E – Motivating the Sales Force

The National Sales Manager will motivate the sales force by providing, in addition to the remuneration plan, all the job satisfactions required by upwards of fifty people, each of whom derives his/her job satisfactions from differing sources. Keep him/herself 'tuned' to the morale of the sales force and sense problems almost before they arise, planning and executing the necessary action to avoid low-morale conditions and to maintain a highly motivated sales team.

Standards of performance in relation to the above are met when:

(a) the sales force is kept fully informed on company happenings, changes, new polices, the stock situation, price changes, in a quickly produced sales bulletin, sent out every Monday

(b) the same bulletin includes at least three 'application feedback' reports, giving the fullest credit to the sales executives who supplied the reports

(c) the same bulletin includes frequent mention of sales executives by name related to specific attainments, or to activity over and above the accepted line of duty

(d) a spirit of competitiveness is introduced – between individuals and between regions – and when the weekly bulletin is wisely used to promote this spirit

(e) the top twenty sales executives are listed in the bulletin each week (or month)

(f) all regional sales managers are holding regular monthly sales meetings where the major objective is to motivate and enthuse

(g) the national sales manager holds monthly meetings with his/her regional sales manager, where the major objective is to motivate and enthuse

(h) 10% of the sales promotional budget is appropriated to 'sell' the company and its products to the sales force

(i) the queries and/or complaints of the sales force are dealt with rapidly and fairly, when the national sales manager takes care to ensure he/she is in possession of all the facts, and where decisions, even if unpopular, are seen to be fair and for the overall good of the company

(j) the backup services of the company are seen by the sales force to be marketing orientated and of a high state of efficiency.

F – Selling to National Accounts

The National Sales Manager will sell to national accounts as specified. Negotiate annual contracts. Direct regional sales managers and sales executives to provide effective coverage of all national account outlets

Standards of performance in relation to the above are met when:

(a) National accounts award annual contracts to the company on the basis of product and service quality rather than on the basis of price alone

(b) the growth rate of the national account business is in line with the marketing plan

G – Relationships

The National Sales Manager is accountable to the marketing director for the proper interpretation and fulfilment of his/her basic function. He/she will act in an advisory capacity towards all other members of top management whenever matters pertaining to the sales organisation arise. He/she may delegate to appropriate members of staff certain responsibilities with the corresponding authority, but must keep him/ herself informed on all matters of importance and may not delegate his overall responsibility for results or any portion of his accountability.

Sample Job Description
for a Managing Director

Job title: Managing director, UK Widgets Ltd.

Reporting to: Vice-president Marketing, Universal Widget Corporation.

Liaising with: Moulded Widgets Ltd (managing director), Widgets SA France (managing director)

Function: Overall responsibility for the profitable management of UK Widgets Ltd.

Geographic area: All UK and Eire.

Group Management Meetings:

Attendance at monthly management meetings with associate group companies is mandatory.

Duties:

1 – Marketing

- To achieve a high market share in volume and value.
- To maximise price levels consistent with market share and volume.
- To appraise constantly and update marketing policies.
- To review economic data relevant to markets on a consistent basis.
- To review market trends, competitive activity and general market data.
- To develop and update all advertising, promotional activities and product literature.
- To maintain customer service in respect of sales administration, distribution stocks and spares inventory, relative to sales forecasts.
- To develop sound relationships with relevant trade associations, professional and technical bodies operating in the UK.
- To develop sales for present products into new markets.
- To obtain and maintain a wide range of live business contacts.
- To provide vigour in the sales force.

2 – Financial

- To ensure that all company activities are coordinated with the financial controller and that all reports and returns required by company law are filed in due time.

- To maintain under strict surveillance all cost/profit contributions on a regular basis.
- To keep a watching brief on cost trends.
- To control and anticipate overhead expenses using planned budgets.
- To ensure all costing systems have instant update.
- To review debtors on a minimum monthly basis.
- To control inventory levels.
- To provide adequate space for planned inventory.
- To shed unprofitable products.
- To maintain the group's price leadership philosophy.
- To produce all necessary budgets and forecasts.

3 – Production/Product Development

- To maintain and enhance product quality.

- To ensure that production units (own and subcontract) have sales forecasts.

- To maintain a review of end users and specifiers of Widgets in all markets.

- To improve the present range of products.

- To develop a more effective produce mix.

- To develop a more effect market mix.

- To develop new products for new markets.

- To coordinate existing products and new products.

- To ensure that a monthly report covering marketing, finance and production/ product development is submitted to the Vice-President Marketing

4 – Purchasing

- To ensure that products and materials required for UK Widgets Ltd are procured from reliable, cost-effective and technically competent sources.

5 – Personnel

- To recruit management personnel and to delegate to them duties as required.
- To attract to and maintain at UK Widgets Ltd top-quality management and staff.
- To remunerate and motivate above-average people at above-average levels as an investment in long-term performance.
- To develop future managers for expanding operations elsewhere in Universal Widget Corporation.
- To maintain a good working environment.
- To update terms and conditions of employment in line with current legislation.
- To develop on a continuous basis an improved organisational structure.

6 – Legal

- To take appropriate legal advice on all relevant matters, and to refer to fellow directors and Vice-president Marketing on these relevant matters.
- To be watchful and defensive of the company's patents, registered designs, copyrights and trade names.
- To maintain a strictly legal posture in dealing with employees, suppliers, customers, trade unions, local authorities and government departments.

7 – Planning

- To ensure that adequate medium and long-range plans are produced for products in:
    - (a)   the motor vehicle widget market
    - (b)   the aerospace widget market
    - (c)   the civil engineering widget market.
- To perceive new needs and opportunities and to prepare and submit plans accordingly to the Vice-president Marketing.

NOTE: Managing directors who also perform the function of sales manager need to knit these last two sample job specifications together to make one. Do you want any better reason to start looking for a sales manager? It's better than a coronary.

K

Key Tasks

All sales managers who are doing the job properly will, in their own way, be following a four-step cycle of key tasks. However, within the cycle, there are a number of vital tasks or functions that the sales manager should be performing:

Leading and Motivating

(a)   Sales meetings
(b)   Field visits with sales people
(c)   Counselling
(d)   Contests
(e)   Recognition
(f)   Human relations
(g)   Providing job satisfaction

Training

(a)   Basic training – new sales people
(b)   Continuous training (formal)
(c)   Use of outside consultants
(d)   Identification of training needs
(e)   Measurement of training results
(f)   Role playing
(g)   On the job (field) training

Controlling

(a)   Systems
(b)   Sales activity control
(c)   Sales results control
(d)   Project control
(e)   Blue chip account control
(f)   Sales cost control

Communicating

(a)   Telephone contact with sales people
(b)   Telephone contact with other managers
(c)   Written communications with sales people and managers
(d)   Weekly sales bulletin
(e)   Weekly product bulletin
(f)   Leading and Attending sales meetings
(g)   Sales conferences
(h)   Reports

Ideally, the sales manager should be as free as possible from administrative responsibilities. These can easily be organised under a competent sales office manager reporting to the marketing director. The vital skills of a sales manager are those of leading, training, motivating and controlling and if he or she is good at the job (as they should be) it's folly to load him or her with administration details.

Too much administration blunts the sales manager's effectiveness in the field and doesn't allow his or her talents to be concentrated on producing the optimum results.

Another factor to be considered is that (often) the best sales managers are not suited to administrative tasks. These are best under the control of a good marketing person. Such a person usually possesses a different type of brain to that of a sales manager. They are usually able to give more attention to detail and they probably have an extensive training, enabling them to properly organise the administrative side of the department.

Knowledge Needs

Providing the input to satisfy your salespeoples' knowledge needs is a task many sales managers neglect. At the beginning of the salesperson's job, the induction training programme must include all the information he/she needs to successfully do the job. And KNOWLEDGE is entirely different from SKILLS.

The *knowledge* needed to succeed in Selling includes:

(a) Knowledge of the products or services to be sold

(b) Their applications

(c) The competition – everything about THEIR products or services (how else can you 'sell the difference'?)

(d) The Customers' business

(e) The Customers' markets

(f) Relevant legal aspects

(g) How money makes the (business) world go round.

(h) How to read and interpret a set of accounts

After the initial knowledge input, this sort of information has to be updated REGULARLY. That means MEETINGS and TRAINING.

L

Leadership

Right at the beginning of this book, I said that probably somebody in your organisation had recognised your abilities – they had seen in you some of the attributes that would make a good sales manager.

Well, almost certainly, one of the main attributes they recognised was your potential to become a leader. Perhaps you weren't a leader at the time, but there was something indefinable about you, something that suggested you had somewhere inside, the essential qualities of leadership.

The only problem is, nobody yet has been able to define leadership exactly.

A leader has vision – is able to see into the future and to see what is possible. But more than that, a leader is able to persuade other people of his or her vision and is able to guide them to its realisation.

Broken down into its parts, leadership turns out to be made up of a number of qualities. Some people have those qualities and use them well to become good leaders; others have the same qualities and are not good leaders. Some have the qualities but don't even want to be leaders.

One of the major arguments about leadership is whether leaders are born or made. Well, whatever you are going to attain in this life, it helps to be born first. But whether born or made, there's no doubt leadership can be 'developed'.

There are four things that make leadership work:

1. The leader must have a clear vision of the objective/s to be attained by both him/herself and his or her followers.

2. The leader must have a good idea of how the objective or purpose may be attained.

3. Members of the group must share the leader's vision and all must have a common purpose.

4. The authority of the leader must be freely accepted by all members of the group.

One well-known leadership concept is Action Centred Leadership (ACL) developed by Dr John Adair. ACL focuses on three elements:

(a) achieving the task
(b) building the team
(c) satisfying the individual.

Successful leaders (which means successful sales managers) must like people. They must possess good 'people skills'. They will be good at getting the team to work together, yet will also be conscious of each individual in the team. They will possess powerful skills in communications, people development and innovation. They will tend to be democratic and freedom loving, rather than authoritarian and regimented.

They will seek to lead a people-orientated, 'flattened' structure in which the leader does not stick out as the primary focus. Their sales group will be as 'democratic' as possible. They will allow for maximum team contributions.

These elements comprise the modern form of leadership – as opposed to the old fashioned form, which was at best patronising, hierarchical and authoritarian. (*'Grab 'em by the balls and their hearts and minds will follow!'*)

Sales managers who are good leaders will:

(a) Have subordinates that respect rather than fear them.

(b) Allow subordinates in the team to manage themselves as much as possible.

(c) Understand the personal needs of the individuals in their team.

(d) Treat all their people alike and avoid playing favourites.

(e) Know their people and be aware of the difference in their abilities, interests, and personalities.

(f) Encourage suggestions and will insist that all sales staff participate in planning goals and objectives.

(g) Know how to motivate their sales people.

(h) Develop a team spirit – one of mutual cooperation.

(i) Keep the team well informed of any and all changes within the organisation.

(j) Understand the individual training needs of every member of the team and maintain a continual personal development programme.

(k) Regularly appraise performance and supply feedback.

Leadswingers

Absenteeism remains the scourge of British industry. Although factory and shop floor workers are supposed to be the most prone to taking a 'sickie', there are plenty of other jobs and professions where having 'flu' for the day or going (yet again) to granny's funeral is common.

Salespeople are not immune; they too take days off. But, because of the nature of their work, they can go one better. They can go AWOL. And you might never know. It's called skiving.

In the days before mobile phones, in-car laptop computers and the rest of the hi-tech, IT hardware, it was difficult for sales managers to keep track, (though the good ones always managed it). Now it's easier to know where salespeople are and what they're doing. At least most of the time.

It is important that you check from time to time that salespeople are where they are supposed to be – on their territory – **selling**. It doesn't hurt to turn up unannounced now and again. It's called MBDA – management by driving around.

If you have salespeople prone to absenteeism or skiving, let them know you know. Have a word. Maybe they have home or personal problems which are getting in the way of the job. Although you're not a counsellor or psychotherapist, part of your job is to help your (good) people overcome their problems.

If one of your people persists in skiving, go through the verbal and written warning procedures and get rid of them. If one of the team gets away with it, others might think they can too.

If many of the team are frequently sick or caught skiving, think hard. Maybe there is something wrong within the company.

If you develop a feeling in your water that one of your salespeople is not playing fair, then take positive action fast, otherwise the feeling will grow into a cancerous attitude against the person which will insidiously mar your working relationship.

Find out for sure whether he or she takes the kids to school each morning, collects them each afternoon, makes all the calls that the reports claim he or she has, plays golf or goes shopping with his or her friends alternate Wednesdays and Fridays – or whatever.

And if he or she does these things, have them into your office and present them with the facts. Then tell them that they are being a bloody fool, ask them to choose between resigning and doing the job properly, and if he or she decides to carry on, confirm the discussion with a confidential memo.

Check again seven weeks later. If he or she is still leadswinging, or attending interviews for another job, initiate dismissal proceedings. Then call the rest of the team together and tell them all precisely what you have done and why. After that, no one's in any doubt about what will happen to leadswingers in this organisation.

Of course, it follows that school trips, weekday golf, etc, are all out for you.

How do you check up? Well, £200 buys you a good private detective for a week.

League Tables

League tables are one of the best and most commonly used methods of providing performance feedback against key objectives. Don't try to hide the company's true performance from your sales team, or disguise money figures by allocating numbers of units. Play it all straight. Tell everybody the best – and the worst.

League tables can be prepared by data logged onto computer spreadsheets or into databases. They can then be shown on a large screen at a sales meeting, using a small table-top projector.

It's a good idea if possible for the league table to measure more than one key area. It doesn't take too much effort to devise a league table that could, for instance, show:

total calls made	average daily calls
total orders	average value of order
turnover to date	turnover against budget
new prospect calls	new business ... etc.

With modern computer spreadsheets, all of these key performance areas (and even more) can be shown for six, eight, or even more sales people, quite easily.

Don't ever try to hide the company's true performance from your salespeople, or disguise money figures by allocating code numbers or units. Play it straight. Tell everyone the worst – and the best.

Give each salesperson a detailed rundown on his or her sales figures, calls, quotations, leads, ratios, profitability and whatever, at least once a month. Give each salesperson everyone else's figures also. Let everyone see how everyone else is doing.

Only then will you begin to convert the salespeople at the bottom of the league table into self starters. All you need to do after that is keep filling the tank and priming the petrol pump.

The best kind of league table is one which relates to annual targets and which allows the targets to be adjusted as the months progress (not the targets related to commission earnings). The table opposite shows an example of such a league table for a company employing twenty salespeople and having four area sales managers who regularly reassess the business outlook for each of their salespeople.

It is important to tell everybody everyone else's figures. Do not hide anyone's figures – they will only spend time and money finding out via the grape-vine. Include figures for new salespeople as everyone **knows** that they are new.

THE MONTHLY LEAGUE TABLE

This example is for a large sales force with several area managers who also need motivating

RESULTS AT END OF MONTH - 8				AREA MANAGER'S CURRENT ESTIMATE FOR REST OF YEAR		
SALESPERSON	ORIGINAL AGREED ANNUAL TARGET	TURNOVER ACHIEVED SO FAR	BALANCE LEFT TO ACHIEVE	WILL MAKE BALANCE ON NOSE	WILL SELL MORE THAN BALANCE BY	WILL SELL LESS THAN BALANCE BY
Andrews J	150,000	98,000	52,000	✓		
Arnold P	150,000	122,000	28,000	✓		
Beasley G	110,000	108,000	2,000		25,000	
Brewster M	110,000	85,000	25,000	✓		
Carver D	84,000	61,000	23,000	✓		
Evans D	110,000	73,000	37,000			20,000
Gilman R	140,000	80,000	60,000			25,000
Jacobs E	125,000	123,000	2,000		35,000	
Keith B	80,000	58,000	22,000		5,000	
McEwan J	86,000	35,000	51,000			33,000
Norman L	150,000	105,000	45,000	✓		
Onions P	127,000	90,000	37,000			17,000
Packer A	165,000	122,000	43,000			10,000
Porter J	130,000	70,000	60,000			30,000
Roberts G	55,000	36,000	19,000	✓		
Sutcliffe S	102,000	75,000	27,000			7,000
Taylor B	60,000	37,000	23,000		7,000	
Thompson P	110,000	79,000	31,000		2,000	
Vincent W	100,000	85,000	15,000		18,000	
Watson J	150,000	110,000	40,000		5,000	

Note - All figures are rounded up or down to the nearest 1,000

M

Marketing

Customers are the foundation of any company. Without customers, the company collapses.

The purpose of Marketing (and Selling) is to find and satisfy the needs of customers.

How well the company does this is reflected in its profits –

the bottom line.

The function of Marketing is to develop products or services that will satisfy the specific needs of customers in a particular market and supply those products or services at prices that will yield a profit to the company.

Marketing is the delivery of a way of life.

Marketing has the scope and capacity to look and to move in two directions:

> One direction is *before the event* – to produce product or service ideas long before they are manufactured or delivered (or even thought of by customers).

> The other direction is *after the event* – to think about satisfying and maximising customers' use of the product or service long after they've purchased it and to make customers want to buy again and again.

The Marketing Concept

The 'Marketing Concept' is a management process that puts emphasis on the marketing aspects of the whole organisation. In other words, the *raison d' être* of the organisation – it's reason for existence – is the marketing of its products or services. Marketing is not solely about selling goods that already exist. It is also focused on investigating what customers want (even if they're not yet aware that they want it) and producing the goods and services that will satisfy those customers' requirements.

For instance, who knew they wanted a ballpoint pen until ballpoint pens were available to be purchased? What housewife knew a vacuum cleaner was absolutely essential in her life until she saw one advertised.

Marketing embraces everything within the company. Marketing requires the participation, cooperation and coordination of all the major functions in a company in order to satisfy customers.

Sales is the leading edge – the sharp end – of Marketing. It's where representatives of the company meet the customers on a regular basis, not only to sell them the company's products, but also to obtain feedback about the company and developments in the marketplace.

The Chartered Institute of Marketing defines Marketing as 'the management process responsible for identifying, anticipating and satisfying customers' requirements profitably.'

The Marketing Mix

There are various elements within Marketing which need to be carefully employed and balanced in order to achieve maximum success. They have to be combined in an effective and optimum way. The Marketing Mix is:

Promotion
> Advertising (above and below the line)
> Selling
> Public relations
> Brand image

Product

Product design
Quality
After sales service

Price

Pricing policy
Credit policy

Place

Channels of distribution (retail, wholesale, sales agents, direct
sales, etc)
Location of availability
Warehousing

It is obvious that sales is an important part of the Marketing Mix.
What sets it apart is that feedback from the sales force is necessary for
the correct development and decisions to be made in all other areas.

It follows then that if Selling is the tactical expression of the
business, Marketing is the strategy that determines those tactics.
Selling ensures that customers buy what the business offers.
Marketing ensures the business offers what the customers want to buy.

The approach differs in industrial and consumer Marketing:

Industrial Marketing

Most businesses in the industrial sector use the Marketing Mix when
focusing on what needs to be done.

1. Market research
2. Product development
3. Pricing policy
4. Sales promotion
5. Selling
6. Physical distribution
7. After sales service

Consumer Marketing

Most businesses in the consumer or fmcg sectors find the 7 Ps of Marketing suits them better

1. Planning
2. Product
3. Position
4. Pricing
5. Packaging
6. Promotion
7. Placement

How much a sales manager gets involved in each of these elements of Marketing will depend, of course, on his or her job description and responsibilities.

However, every sales manager should have a sound understanding of every element of Marketing, if only to aid communication with other people and departments within the corporate hierarchy.

Mobile Phones

An absolute MUST. No field sales force can do effective business without them in today's traffic gridlock conditions.

Imagine one customer lost because he was kept waiting an hour whilst your salesperson was stuck in a traffic jam with no way of communicating with anyone – that's probably ten times the cost of the mobile phone.

And *every call* is monitored by printout. Nobody can fiddle these.

By far the best hi-tech method of maximising calls and minimising travelling time in any urban area has been made possible by the mobile phone.

The field salesperson drives in the company car (which is still required for all non-urban areas) to an hotel on the outskirts of the day's urban area. Parking the car safely in the hotel carpark, the salesperson (it is too early for the first call) has breakfast in the hotel restaurant and, five minutes before his or her departure time, uses the mobile phone to summon the first taxi of the day.

The company has negotiated running monthly accounts with selected taxi firms in each urban area – 'brown wrappers', not London cabs.

Five minutes after the first tele-call summons, the salesperson walks out of the hotel and into the taxi. During the drive to the first call, he or she does business with his mobile phone.

Five minutes before the salesperson is due to depart the first call, he or she says to the customer, 'Would you mind if I used my mobile phone to ring for my driver? He's about five minutes away.' The customer thinks 'Driver?' and the salesperson goes soaring up in perceived value and status.

Five minutes later, the salesperson is into the second taxi of the day – probably a different one – and on way to the second call, again doing business on the mobile phone during the journey.

And so on through the day, till the last taxi takes the salesperson back to the hotel for a leisurely cup of tea, over which he or she does the paperwork, prior to driving home after the main bulk of the traffic has passed by.

Believe it – this is the lowest cost, maximum business way of doing the business. Maximum calls; no time wasted trying to find places to park; no parking fines; no late appointments and all that extra business from the calls made during the travelling time. Swallow hard and try it for yourself.

Moonlighters

Moonlighters are harder to catch than leadswingers. They either use their energies in pursuing another after-hours job or, worse still, they sell someone else's products at the same time as they are selling yours, and to the same customers.

Do not ever advocate, encourage or allow any form of moonlighting. If a salesperson isn't totally committed to your company, its objectives and his or her target, get rid of them.

I've known salespeople with their own businesses – with dress shops which they run on Saturdays, with fish and chip saloons, with market stalls, who act as barmen every night of the week, who play in dance bands, who sell insurance on the side, who are part-time lecturers at technical colleges, who trade in antiques, jewellery, porn, contraceptives, instant print and who sell advertising space as well as fork-lift trucks.

There are two million known moonlighters in Britain, those who are registered with the Inland Revenue as having two jobs. On the iceberg principle, that means there could be at least sixteen million in total.

Any kind of moonlighting saps your employee's energies and you lose. Make sure all your salespeople are prohibited from carrying on any other kind of business activity by building an appropriate clause into their service contracts.

If you have such a clause, and you catch someone moonlighting, get rid of them. Quickly. And make sure the rest of the team know why.

Motivating the Troops

People are basically 'wanting animals'. A good sales manager recognises this and understands that real motivation comes from within. External factors can influence motivation, either positively or negatively, but the engine of motivation – the mechanism whereby an individual may be motivated – must already be present.

Thankfully it is in almost everybody.

But each 'engine' is as different as the person who owns it.

In good salespeople, the motors of motivation are supercharged, fuel-injection models. A good salesperson has a high-performance engine of wants, desires and needs. That's what makes them go. It's not the sales manager's job to install the engine. It is the sales manager's job to make sure the engine is already present when he or she is recruiting new salespeople.

You can't put the engine into the person. What you can do is fine-tune it, and make it perform to the maximum with the right fuel. Ever tried making a high-performance petrol engine run on diesel?

It's obvious, then, that each individual's motivation is personal to them. So it follows that sales managers need to find out what personally motivates the individual members of the sales teams. There are, however, some basic principles of motivation that apply to most people under most circumstances.

You can tell when people are obviously motivated when they:

    (a) Consistently achieve high performance results

    (b) Have sufficient energy, enthusiasm and determination to overcome obstacles and succeed

    (c) Demonstrate a high level of cooperation with other members of the team

    (d) Show a willingness to accept responsibility

    (e) Show a willingness to accommodate change

A lack of motivation is signalled by:

(a) Apathy and indifference to the job,

(b) Poor time keeping and high absenteeism

(c) An exaggeration of any difficulties which may be encountered in problems and disputes.

(d) A lack of cooperation in their dealings with other members of the team

(e) An unjustified resistance to change.

Change can be a great motivator or de-motivator. Most people say they welcome change. What they mean is they want things to be different whilst staying exactly as they are. Change is often seen as a threat and has to be 'sold'.

Get the motivation going

Motivation may be described as 'having sufficient reason' for doing something.

Nobody ever does something unless he or she has a reason for doing so.

So, to motivate is 'to furnish with a reason or motive', that is 'to make somebody want to do a particular task'.

Tasks are either enjoyable or unpleasant. But, remember, your definition of what is enjoyable, or not, may not necessarily be the salesperson's.

(a) If enjoyable, people will need very little motivation to make them perform the task, or they must face a strong penalty to stop them doing it.

(b) If unpleasant, they will need powerful motivation to carry out the task and very little excuse to avoid doing so.

Therefore management has a basic choice in motivation of either offering some kind of reward for carrying out a task, or of making a threat of some form of penalty for not doing so – the traditional 'carrot' and 'stick' philosophy. But although the 'big stick' may have worked well in years gone by, it is almost totally ineffective in the economic and social environment of today.

This is not to say that 'fear' does not motivate. Used occasionally and selectively, it can prove a spur to the poor performer who has potential to do better; and fear can – and should – be used in disciplinary matters. But when used continuously, it can 'motivate' the best performers to find another job whilst demotivating the others into giving minimum acceptable results.

The following notes outline the most relevant theories of motivation for sales managers and salespeople. They emphasise the need for *positive* motivation:

(a) Motivation is achieved by the promise of satisfaction of individual needs.

(b) Each individual has different needs and wants which may change from week to week and year to year.

(c) Each individual has a different level of drive – the effort which he or she is willing to apply to achieve each need.

(d) Motivation must relate to the promise of something in the future. People are not motivated by things that have already happened.

(e) Group motivation can be based on the common needs of the group but additional attention must be directed to individual needs.

(f) Fear can be used as an occasional short-term motivator but in the long term it leads to friction and dissatisfaction.

(g) Removing any cause of dissatisfaction will not motivate. It will result only in ending the demotivational effect.

(h) There is a level beyond which each individual cannot be motivated. If all needs are reasonably satisfied, further reward has no effect.

Abraham Maslow – The Hierarchy of Needs

One of the first modern researchers into motivation was Abraham Maslow, who suggested that human needs are organised at different levels, and can be classified in a 'hierarchy of needs'. ('Motivation and Personality' 1954) For a clearer grasp of this concept, the five levels of 'needs' should be read from the bottom up, rather than from the top down.

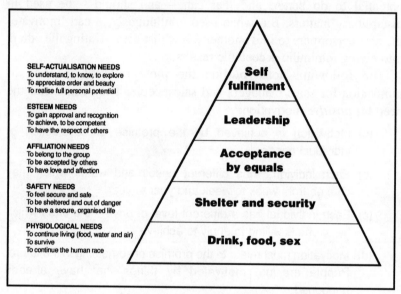

SELF-ACTUALISATION NEEDS
To understand, to know, to explore
To appreciate order and beauty
To realise full personal potential

ESTEEM NEEDS
To gain approval and recognition
To achieve, to be competent
To have the respect of others

AFFILIATION NEEDS
To belong to the group
To be accepted by others
To have love and affection

SAFETY NEEDS
To feel secure and safe
To be sheltered and out of danger
To have a secure, organised life

PHYSIOLOGICAL NEEDS
To continue living (food, water and air)
To survive
To continue the human race

Self fulfilment
Leadership
Acceptance by equals
Shelter and security
Drink, food, sex

Maslow's Hierarchy of Needs

Each individual must be reasonably satisfied *at each level of need* before feeling free to seek satisfaction *at the next level up* – and when a lower level is threatened, attention will revert to that level to 'repair the foundations'.

The lower the level in the hierarchy, the stronger will be the motivational value, so that, in time, hunger and thirst will take overall priority.

Each individual will be motivated by the opportunity to progress upwards in the hierarchy of needs; but each will have different priorities where needs are concerned, and a different degree of drive to attain them.

Furthermore, these individual needs and drives will change with time, maybe even from hour to hour with regard hunger and thirst – or from year to year as a career progresses, family circumstances change, retirement approaches and so on.

In a well-organised peaceful society, people rarely have any physiological or safety needs as active motivators. Maslow found that knowledge workers will be at their most useful to employers when they are reasonably secure at the lower three levels, and are looking for satisfaction of their 'Esteem Needs' – and maybe seeking leadership in a group situation.

Frederick Hertzberg – Motivators and Hygiene Factors

Since Frederick Hertzberg published his first research on motivation in 'Work and the Nature of Man' in 1968, his studies have stimulated a great deal of further research – notably into the factors which motivate sales personnel.

He made extensive studies of 'knowledge workers' to identify the factors which create satisfying and dissatisfying experiences at work, listing those factors which are commonly accepted as having a major influence on workers' motivation.

He analysed (a) the satisfying effect of having each of the factors present, and (b) the dissatisfying effect when they were reduced or totally absent.

Motivators

He gave the term 'motivators' to those factors which produced a strong positive motivation when present, but a lesser, negative value when absent.

This list of motivators included such factors as:

- achievement and the recognition of achievement
- responsibility
- the possibility of personal growth and advancement
- the satisfying nature of the work itself.

Hygiene Factors

He called 'hygiene factors' those which tended to be taken for granted when present, but which were strong demotivators when absent or reduced. This list of potential dissatisfiers included:

- general working conditions
- company policy and administration
- relationships with others at work
- supervision
- status
- salary and security
- and aspects of personal life.

The hygiene factors tend to be the commercial equivalents of the lower three levels of Maslow's hierarchy – the physiological, safety and love (affiliation) needs. The motivators correspond to the upper needs for esteem and self-fulfilment.

To further clarify this difference:

1. For example, if a person at work is given an increasing level of responsibility, this will motivate that person to greater efforts; if not given that increase, demotivation will not necessarily apply to the same extent.

2. If an individual is reasonably content with the basic salary received, then this will not be a particularly strong motivational factor, but if underpaid – or if others are being paid more for similar work – then this will cause powerful demotivation.

A distinction should be made between 'salary' and financial incentives such as commission or bonus. Salary tends to be taken for granted as a hygiene factor.

Incentives or bonuses can be regarded as recognition of results, and hence as motivators.

Recognising the Signs of Demotivation

The signs of negative motivation or dissatisfaction are progressively:

Aggression – against individuals or perhaps against the company
Regression – childish, petty or spiteful behaviour
Obsession – often (but not always) with the cause of dissatisfaction
Resignation – becoming resigned to the situation with apparent disinterest

Thus the first sign of demotivation may be the appearance of aggression in someone who is not normally aggressive. If the cause of dissatisfaction is not removed, then the next stage (petty or childish behaviour) will start to appear. It is obvious that the condition will become increasingly difficult to rectify as it develops and that it is vital to recognise and act on the early signs.

The manager must remember that the demotivation may not be due to the job situation, but may have been caused by personal or domestic factors. This emphasises the need to know staff well, and treat them as individuals.

Correction of Dissatisfiers

If any of the hygiene factors is considered by the worker to be less than acceptable, this will cause demotivation – and any such dissatisfactions must be corrected to a reasonable extent before any positive motivation can begin.

But such correction will not, in itself, necessarily create motivation: an increase in salary will only remove the source of dissatisfaction. The person will not become happy – he or she will only cease to be unhappy.

Positive Motivation

The traditional approach to motivation – providing better working conditions, greater job security, and so on, relate to hygiene factors;

they are important in avoiding dissatisfaction – but this is all they are likely to achieve.

Positive motivation can be achieved only by concentrating on positive factors:

ACHIEVEMENT   RECOGNITION   RESPONSIBILITY
ADVANCEMENT   PERSONAL GROWTH

Management Style

Management style is obviously closely related to motivation. The style of the manager can either motivate or demotivate the sales team.

If the sales manager recognises that people can be self-motivating, then he or she will be keen to create conditions at work which allow self-motivation. Much of the success of this depends upon the manager's attitude – his or her style in relation to his or her people and the assumptions he or she makes about people at work.

Douglas McGregor, in 'The Human Side of Enterprise' (McGraw Hill, 1960), produced Theory X and Theory Y concerning attitudes to people at work. Managers' styles are very much based upon which attitude they adopt. Whichever attitude is adopted has a high impact on the motivation of sales team.

The X-Y Theory

Theory X says that people *dislike* work:

   (a) People dislike work and will avoid it if they can

   (b) People must be forced or bribed to put out the right effort

   (c) People would rather be directed than accept responsibility, which they avoid

   (d) People are motivated mainly by money

   (e) People are motivated by anxiety about security

   (f) Most people have little creativity – except when getting around management rules

Theory Y says that people *enjoy* work:

(a) Work is necessary to people's psychological growth

(b) People want to be interested in their work and, under the right conditions, they enjoy it

(c) People will direct themselves towards an accepted target

(d) People will seek, and accept responsibility under the right conditions

(e) The discipline a person imposes on him- or herself is more effective, and can be more severe, than any imposed on them

(f) Under the right conditions, a person is motivated by the desire to realise their own potential

(g) Creativity and ingenuity are widely distributed and grossly under-used

If the sales manager adopts and 'buys into' McGregor's Theory Y, certain things will be obvious in their style:

- They will always lead by example
- They will treat all their sales staff with dignity, not as objects or as sales machines.
- They will not discriminate among their people on any basis other than competence in the job, e.g. they will have no sexual, racial, religious, or any other kind of discrimination
- They will emphasise 'we' and minimise 'I'
- They will not believe they are personally or innately superior to the sales team. They will simply recognise that they have different responsibilities
- They will be loyal to their staff
- They will not rationalise or seek to excuse their own mistakes, but they will learn from them and carry on
- They will not constantly seek to be the centre of attention. They will allow others to take the credit and permit them to bask in any glory, without feeling slighted
- They will not say anything derogatory about the organisation or people in it.

- They will not lose their cool
- They will not take precipitant action when angry. They will wait until they have an objective view of the situation
- They will seek to build up the sale team
- They will not build themselves up by tearing others down
- They will not use foul language (even when irritated).

A manager who believes absolutely in either Theory X or Theory Y is actually believing in a caricature at either end of a scale or continuum. Most managers could set their own beliefs somewhere between the two extremes.

Once your personal position is found along the continuum and is recognised by colleagues and staff, any substantial or unexpected deviation from that position can cause alarm, puzzlement and disaffection amongst your team.

Just occasionally, you may need to shift temporarily closer towards Theory X, as for instance, when you need to exert more authority or discipline. Likewise, a drift towards the Theory Y end is permissible (in fact, even valuable) when you are seeking the team's approval for a more difficult decision.

Getting rid of "I Can't Win With This One!"

A sales manager I know who runs a large salesforce has a one-off exercise aimed at changing a particular kind of subconscious negative thinking back to conscious positive thinking. He calls it the 'I can't win with this guy' feeling. It comes to quite a lot of salespeople after they've tried for an appointment, say, three or four times and have received a blunt 'No' each time. The occasion we heard of when he exercised (or should it be exorcised) his salesforce went like this.

He called all fifty of his salespeople together for half a day, telling them to bring all their customer and prospect records with them. They were all seated around a big, hollow square table, the sales manager walking about most of the time. There was a bit of general business to get through, which took the first hour – then he gave his instructions:

"Sort out from your prospect record cards the six worst prospects you've got – people who you know are good prospects, yet with whom you haven't got even to first base."

When each of his fifty salespeople had done this, he gave his next instruction:

"Now, each of you pass the six cards you're holding to the person on your immediate right."

This they each did. Then the sales manager pointed to the clock on the wall and shouted:

"Right, you have two hours to get out of here, every one of you, find a phone and get a firm appointment with those six prospects you're now holding in your hand. GO!"

All fifty sat dumbstruck. "He can't be serious!" they were saying to themselves.

"GO!" the sales manager thundered. "Two hours – no more."

They went, initially just a trickle, then a rush which turned into a stampede, and the fifty salespeople were gone.

Three hours later, not two, they were all back in the room, once more seated around the square. Scores were totted up, and to everyone's amazement, the overall success rate was 160 appointments out of a possible 300. More than 50% success – much better than normal performance in the field. And these were the worst possible known prospects.

On the analysis, four key reasons for this success were established:

(a) The salespeople had no preconceived failure complexes in their subconscious. The prospects they telephoned were unknown to them.

(b) They had maximum enthusiasm for the task, because they took it as a personal challenge from a sales manager they respected (that's leadership!).

(c) They had a second challenge, perhaps more powerful to some than the first, that of proving to a colleague who had failed that they could succeed.

(d) Most of the successful 160 were telephone calls where the name of the salesperson who had passed on the six cards to the caller was used by the caller, as a third party reference. 'Your name has been given to me by one of my colleagues, Joe Randolph. He reckons we've a deal coming up that could save you a fair bit of money. Could you spare me ten minutes, say on Wednesday, for me to come over and talk to you about it?'

The 'deal' they invented. The objective was to secure the appointment. They discovered that the name of one of their own salespeople was almost as effective as the name of one of their customers. They had plenty of time to think about what best to say and do when they arrived face-to-face.

So much for the subconscious negative trap. Few of this particular salesforce ever suffered from it again – and, from time to time, they continued swapping 'difficult' prospect cards.

The **SIX** most important words:

'I ADMIT I MADE A MISTAKE'

the **FIVE** most important words:

'YOU DID A GOOD JOB'

the **FOUR** most important words:

'WHAT IS YOUR OPINION?'

the **THREE** most important words:

'WOULD YOU MIND?'

the **TWO** most important words:

'THANK YOU'

the **ONE** most important word:

'WE'

the **LEAST** important word:

'I'

N

Negotiating

As a salesperson, now elevated to the position of sales management, you already know how to sell. Perhaps as a salesperson, you were also involved in negotiating with national accounts and/or major customers. Even as a sales manager, you may well be continuing to negotiate large or national account customers.

What is different now is that much of your negotiating will be internal – with colleagues and other departmental heads within the organisation. It's useful, therefore, to remind yourself of the principles of negotiating and to understand how they apply to internal negotiations.

The first things to remember is that, with internal negotiations *you live with the outcome of your negotiations every day.*

You are unlikely to be negotiating the sale of a product or service internally. Frequently the matter will be more intangible – perhaps negotiating a larger or different office space, or whether your department gets first bite at the latest computer hardware/software or new office furniture, or whatever.

You could be negotiating for a better type of car for your sales force or a better bonus or incentive scheme. You may be negotiating with your secretary when she demands an increase in salary. You may be negotiating your own salary.

Because of your sales experience, it's likely you will be a better negotiator that many of your colleagues. This could mean that you're able to pull off an absolute triumph in any bargaining.

Resist the temptation.

Always try to make your negotiations win-win. Just like sales negotiations. Resist the temptation to go for the throat or deliver the *coup de grâce.*

Why? Because you've got to live with the people you defeated. If you inflict a crushing defeat on a colleague in a negotiation – he or she will remember it. They will be looking for ways of getting their own back – of sabotaging you.

The best negotiations are where both sides come out with what they view to be more or less a satisfactory outcome. Just like sales negotiations.

An imposed settlement, or one where one side is 'sold a pup', always induces resentment. Only men with guns or people selling 'hookey' gear on market stalls can make someone 'an offer they can't refuse'.

There are three major steps in negotiating:

1. **Preparation**
2. **The negotiation itself**
3. **Monitoring the implementation**

Preparation

The more you are prepared in detail, the more likely you are to win (defined as getting the maximum you could reasonably expect from the negotiations). Therefore you need to:

(a) Define in absolute detail what you want to achieve – your overall objective.

(b) Define the minimum position you are prepared to accept – the point beyond which you will have to abandon the negotiations.

(c) Define your own strengths – your bargaining power – and compare it to the other side's.

(d) If your bargaining position or power is obviously less than that of the other side – seek to delay the negotiations until your position can be strengthened.

(e) Prepare your case carefully and in detail. Document as much as you can. Make sure you and everybody else on your team is completely briefed.

The Negotiation

1. Try to get the other side to do most of the talking in the opening moves of the negotiations. Get them to explain their position in detail and obtain as much information as possible about their arguments. Be on the lookout for holes and inconsistencies.

2. Listen to the words – and listen also for the 'music'. Often what people say isn't what they mean, or believe. Listen for the tone of voice and observe the body language. Try to assess how willing they are to shift from their position.

3. At the same time, conceal, as far as reasonable, your own position.

4. Redefine your opponent's views or position, putting it in your own words. This may help them to make a shift from their present position towards one which benefits you.

5. Always be ready for the possibility of an early settlement – usually when events are going in your favour.

6. When you have reached a settlement, document the agreement in detail. Although this may be the responsibility of someone keeping the minutes of the meeting, don't rely on the minutes. Always produce and circulate your own understanding of the agreement you've reached.

7. After getting the other side to outline their position in detail, look for ways in which, *without aggression*, you can:

    (a) undermine their arguments by challenging their assumptions

    (b) dispute their facts and show up any major inconsistencies

    (c) undermine their credibility

    (d) question their experience or expertise

    (e) support your own position and credibility by showing you have a mastery of the detail.

    (f) appeal to reason

    (g) if things are at an impasse, get the other side to move their position by summing up what has been said so far and suggesting that it is now time for concessions

(h) suggest a new position – which means changing positions for both sides – though considerably less for you

(i) link or 'bundle' two or more issues together – one being reliant upon the other

(j) encourage the other side to abandon some of their positions by outlining the concessions you may make

(k) suggest circumstances have changed

(l) identify their misunderstandings.

Monitoring the Implementation

This is often the trickiest part of the whole proceedings. Some people will agree things in a negotiation which they have no intention of implementing.

Don't let them do it ... and don't do it yourself.

Insist they stick with the deal or you must open up the negotiations again.

Set up a system of monitoring which has been agreed in advance.

John Winkler, the well known expert on negotiating, suggests a number of tips in bargaining. The following is based on his recommendations:

1. If you don't have to negotiate, don't. If you can get what you want without having to give anything away – why negotiate?

2. Be prepared.

3. Let the other side do the work. It's worth making a significant demand early in the negotiation and sticking with it, or as close as you can. This forces the other side to work harder to squeeze concessions from you.

4. Apply pressure gently, building it up slowly. Ensure you have lots of shots in your locker.

5. Make them compete

6. Leave yourself space. Allow yourself room for manoeuvre. Ask for more than you expect, but concede less than you are actually prepared to give.

7. Always remember your minimum negotiating position

8. Maintain your integrity. *Never ever lie.* If you make a commitment, stick to it. Be tough certainly, even cunning, but always be trustworthy.

9. Listen more than talk.

10. Stay with the game. Keep in close touch with where the opposition is currently at – their position.

11. Watch out when making big demands. There's always a limit to how much you can demand without blowing the whole process.

12. Float big demands gently. Bear in mind what you guess must be their minimum position.

13. Give them time – let them get used to your demands. Go for your absolute top limit early and do not give way easily. The other side may be prepared to accept your demands, but it may take them time to get used to them. Be patient.

O

Objectives

An objective that isn't quantified and programmed into a time scale is no more than a wish – a hope – a fantasy.

This applies both to the objectives you set for the sales force and the personal objectives you set for your career advancement.

An objective to substantially increase sales is useless. It's woolly, undefined, unfocussed. How can you hit a target that's no more than a blur?

On the other hand, an objective to achieve sales by x amount by increasing the sales force's call rate by y amount whilst increasing the average value of order by z amount – and by a set date – is both specific and quantified. Written down, it becomes prescriptive; it can be understood by everybody and progress towards it can be monitored. Written objectives, quantified and in a time frame, are easier to achieve.

An objective to reduce customer complaints is, again, just a vague hope.

To achieve a 25% reduction in the average number of customer complaints, within a six-month period, is a specific objective that can be monitored. Plans can be made as to how this is to be achieved.

When it comes to your own, personal, career development, if you have an objective of earning more money, then it is imperative you specify how much and by what date. Then you can think through the steps you need to take in order to achieve your objective.

Even objectives which at first sight appear unquantifiable can be quantified and written down.

For instance, you may have the objective to improve sales force morale. Okay, how can you quantify morale?

You could circulate a survey/questionnaire among the sales force that gets the salespeople to identify areas of current dissatisfaction. Thus you identify the problems. You decide as your objective to halve dissatisfaction in four of the major problem areas within the next month. How?

Perhaps you could improve morale by having a light-hearted weekly newsletter, highlighting new product developments, individuals who have exceeded target, humorous stories from the field and so on. You could double the number of sales meetings and send out plenty of 'well done' and 'thank you' letters. Six months later you can re-circulate the questionnaire to see how close you have come to your objective.

Organising Sales Conferences

Most companies hold an annual sales conference. Some hold them semi-annually. They usually look both forward and back, analysing the performance of the last sales period before going on to plans for the next. Directors, managers and other people within the company talk about various subjects and, sometimes, a couple of visiting speakers may be brought in from outside to give a fresh approach to some sales point or other.

Alternatively (or in addition), the company may run an annual sales training session and use its own management (and others) to do the training. Either way, two or three days are involved and the entire sales force has to be accommodated around the venue for the duration of the event.

If you get stuck with organising the conference, treat it exactly as you would an exhibition – in other words as a project. Although you may be solely responsible for the conference, you will have to liaise with colleagues and outside contractors. Plan backwards from the conference date. And remember – a successful sales conference is as important to the company as a successful exhibition.

Several important factors contribute to a successful conference.

The first is to gain the maximum amount of participation from all the people there. Without this, the ultimate objective – that everyone should go away from the conference totally committed to the plans discussed and firmly believing that they are right – will never be attained.

Conferences should not be used as an opportunity for management to lean heavily on the sales force. Any form of oppression should be avoided.

Oppression can manifest itself in various forms. Trapped within the four walls of the conference venue, a salesperson can feel intimated by his or her surroundings, switch to the defensive and shut up like a clam for the entire proceedings. The conference then becomes demotivating and the money spent on it a complete waste.

All companies are different of course, but there are some general rules for running conferences:

Avoid Having Them on Company Premises

Few companies have the right facilities for a successful conference. The time wasted shuttling back and forth for meals and sorting out accommodation in nearby hotels, usually costs as much as if the company had put the entire proceedings into the right sort of hotel in the first place.

Select the Right Sort of Hotel

Of course, cost is an important factor, but the cost difference between a good and a bad hotel is insignificant when compared with the value of increased business which the company wants the conference delegates to commit to. A bad hotel can ruin a whole year's motivation and performance.

When booking reservations for a conference, never rely solely on the telephone. Go and see for yourself.

The right sort of hotel should have the following facilities:

(a) Single bedrooms with en-suite bathrooms. (Makes the sales force look forward to the event)

(b) A really good restaurant. (The way to a man's heart may be through his stomach – but a lot of women, and quite a few men, like vegetarian food and fresh salads, particularly at lunch time).

(c) really comfortable chairs in the conference room (the mind can only absorb as much as the behind can endure), and tables – something to work and lean on.

(d) The right shaped conference room – and large enough, with plenty of air. If in doubt, always double the size and never choose a low ceiling height. (See under 'Room Layout').

(e) Good visual aids. (Everything from flip charts to the latest computer-linked projectors, with effective blackout, good lighting, microphones, etc). Better than this – employ an A/V firm to build you a stage set and run the technical bits for you. Use radio mikes if your audience is 50 or more, the kind that leave both your hands free.

(f) Venue staff that know about the conference business. (Nothing can break a conference organiser's heart quicker than having hotel staff that hasn't a clue what a good conference needs)

(g) Silence. (Never pick a hotel on a main trunk road, or in the centre of a town. If in doubt, stay for a night yourself and see)

Get the Room Layout Right

There's a hotel in the Midlands that recently spent £1,000,000 on a new conference wing. I will never use it. Whoever designed the new wing clearly had no idea of how a good conference should be run. The 'sharp end' of the room, where the speaker stands, has superb picture windows. Did you ever try to focus on a speaker on a summer afternoon when he or she is standing in front of dazzling sunlight? The strain is tremendous and the audience can't see a thing.

Also, the entrances to the conference room are close to the picture windows. So anyone creeping in and out can be seen by the entire audience. Another concentration sapper. It may sound petty to you, but it really is very important.

For a really effective conference or training session, the audience should face a specially designed set, on a stage, with any audio/visual projection being back-projected, not front.

This means that, if you are using audio-visual aids (video or slide projection), you need another 25 feet of room space behind the stage set for all the technical equipment. Windows should preferably be behind the audience, so the delegates aren't constantly tempted to gaze out at what's going on in the world outside the conference. The only objects in front of delegates should be the speaker and his or her visual aids. Entrances should always be at the back of the room. Whoever is the conference organiser will be in and out all the time, sorting out minor details.

If you are using video equipment, the bottom of the screen must be no less than five feet from the floor, otherwise the back half of your audience will only be able to see the top half of the screen. So, if you're using a 9 x 6 screen, you'll need a ceiling height of at least twelve feet, (fifteen is better) allowing for screen and set assembly.

Always provide your delegates with tables. I have seen so many conferences where the delegates sat theatre-style for three whole days. Nowhere to write notes, nowhere to lean elbows and ease the aching behind. Disaster.

The optimum layout of tables and chairs is as shown opposite. Nobody in the room has to angle his head or body more than forty-five degrees either way to see everything going on at the front.

Allow at least three feet of table per person, and make sure there is plenty of fresh water available for all.

The Conference Programme

Try to split the entire proceedings into sessions of not more than an hour's duration. Use training videos between formal sessions so that the day's work is as varied as possible. If the day starts at 0900 hours, have a coffee break at about 1100 hours and lunch at about 1300 hours. A tea break at about 1600 hours then leaves only two hours before normal finishing time.

If the conference goes on into the evenings, break for dinner early and then go back afterwards. But try not to have any really heavy stuff for the after-dinner business. The levels of concentration will be only half what they were in the morning. A syndicate exercise is best.

As organiser, it is your job to make sure the drinking water is changed at each break, 0900, 1100, 1300, 1600 and 1800. A good hotel staff will automatically do this, but don't rely on them for the first day, just in case.

Take coffee and tea in another room, so that all the participants can stretch their legs. After lunch, insist that each delegate takes a walk around the hotel to get some fresh air. It makes all the difference to the number of yawns during the afternoon.

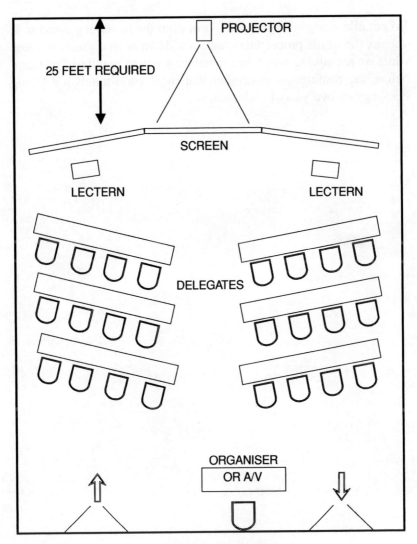

Suggested room layout

Keep to the Timetable

Do not allow anyone to overrun – not even the managing director. If you do, the whole proceedings can come down around your ears. And while we are talking about the timetable, and your months of planning before the conference, remember that most good hotels are taking bookings up two years in advance.

P

Performance Improvement

Most sales managers would say that measuring and monitoring a salesperson's performance or effectiveness is one of the most difficult and most elusive things to get your teeth into.

Not so. It's the way they try to measure and monitor which makes the job difficult. Done properly, monitoring personal performance is one of the easiest jobs the sales manager has to do, and one of the least time consuming.

I've spent more than 20 years developing systems for sales force control, and in this section I'm going to discuss what I consider is the best way of tackling the job.

Basic Principle

A sales force control, measuring or monitoring system must use numbers, not words.

All you can do with words is read them. You can't add them up, multiply them, divide them, cumulate them or anything. So all you get with words is an instant picture of today or yesterday. No sales manager has a computer for a mind, so you cannot correlate all the words you receive from your salespeople and put together an ongoing picture. You'd go mad if you tried.

You cannot judge the performance of a salesperson solely on the turnover produced in a given period of time, or the number of calls made each week. Personal performance measurement needs to cover much more. Here's the most effective way of doing the job properly.

Each week, every salesperson submits to you a list of all the face-to-face calls made during the week, and what happened on each call. This list does not include telephone calls.

This weekly list is in the form shown opposite and is entitled 'Call Analysis'. The design of the form reduces writing to a minimum. Each call takes up one line, most of the 'what happened' data being recorded as ticks. The sections covering 'industry category' and 'product groups discussed' use a master code devised by the company and common to all the salespeople.

Our example shows the calls J. Watson made during week 14 of the year in question. Watson travelled 245 miles to make the calls, and (bottom left) succeeded in submitting two proposals on prospects (not to be confused with existing customers) during the week.

You will receive one of these forms from each of your salespeople in each Monday's post along with expense claims and call plans for the next week. All you do with the information is enter the totals on four master cards you keep for each salesperson. The work of entering the totals on these cards each Monday takes a few minutes only. In fact, your secretary should do it.

Pages 178 and 179 show the two master cards for J. Watson. Following the numbers through from our example of his week 14 call analysis form, you will see where the totals are entered in the week 14 lines on these two cards.

Four items of information must be supplied each week from headquarters (usually accounts) to complete each salesperson's cards. These items are the total orders received from existing customers during the week from each salesperson's territory and the total value of these orders, and likewise for prospects.

The two master cards are designed to calculate performance on a quarterly basis, which has been found by far the most suitable period, being long enough to iron out any abnormalities in the numbers due to holidays or illness and short enough to give the company time to sort out any major problems the numbers pinpoint before these problems get out of hand.

WEEKLY CALL ANALYSIS

WEEK No. **14** — SALESPERSON **J. WATSON**

IF A CALL RESULTS IN "ABORTIVE" STILL TICK THE COLUMNS WHICH INDICATE WHAT KIND OF CALL IT SHOULD HAVE BEEN

PRODUCT GROUPS DISCUSSED (Remember Windows of Opportunity)

DATE	COMPANY CALLED ON	Industry Category	Abortive	Call on Existing Users	Call on Prospect	First Ever Call	Follow up of Lead	Appointment	Requested EU Quotes	Requested P Quotes	Call Report	Order Secured	Service Call	A	B	C	D	E	F	G	H	I	J	K	L	M	N	O	P
M	PORTERHOUSE	2		✓		✓		✓			✓	✓			✓	✓						✓						
	POTTERSBY	2	✓	✓	✓							✓																	
	J & B ENGS	1		✓	✓	✓		✓			✓	✓			✓	✓			✓	✓									
	HEREFORDS	4	✓	✓	✓	✓		✓			✓	✓																	
T	EATON	3		✓										✓															
	WYMAN WELDING	2		✓	✓	✓		✓														✓						
	IBE	4		✓	✓	✓	✓	✓			✓								✓									
	SMITH-DAVIDSON	2		✓			✓								✓	✓	✓			✓									
	FISHER	4		✓											✓														
W	WADES	2		✓																									
	AUTOLIFT	1		✓	✓	✓		✓												✓	✓		✓						
	VICTORIA FORGE	1	✓	✓	✓		✓											✓	✓	✓	✓								
T	ASH & CO	1		✓								✓								✓		✓							
	SMALL & SMALL	4	✓	✓							✓	✓				✓													
	EXHALL TOOLS	2		✓				✓	✓			✓	✓										✓						
F	JONES & PLATT	1		✓	✓	✓		✓								✓	✓												
	BREEDON SMITH	1		✓	✓	✓	✓	✓			✓	✓	✓			✓			✓	✓	✓								
	ARUNDEL DEVELS	2		✓												✓			✓	✓	✓								
	TOTALS		4	12	6 9	5	3	11	1	2	7	5	0	1	4	5	0	3	2	7	2	2						
			1	2 3 4	5 6 7	8	9	10 11	12	13 14	15	16 17	18 19 20	A	B	C	D	E	F	G	H	I	J	K	L	M	N	O	P

INDUSTRY CATEGORY TOTALS

1	2	3	4
6	6	1	4

BUSINESS MILES FOR WEEK **245**

PERSONAL PERFORMANCE RECORD
SECOND QUARTER

YEAR 1999 SALESPERSON J. WATSON

OVERALL

WEEK	MILEAGE	MILES PER CALL RATIO / CUMULATIVES		TOTAL CALLS	ABORTIVE CALL RATIO / CUMULATIVES		NO INTER-VIEW
14	245			18			4
15	240			24			5
16	235			25			2
17	168			20			6
18	196			24			4
19	247			26			1
20	188			24			3
21	304			26			5
22	200			24			4
23	86			10			3
24	210			26			1
25	175			20			1
26	166	2660	288	21	288	44	5
		9.2			6.5		
					8.0		
					COMPANY NORM		

EXISTING CUSTOMERS

TOTAL CALLS ON USERS	CALLS TO ORDER RATIO / CUMULATIVES		TOTAL ORDERS RCD FROM USERS	AVERAGE ORDER VALUE REPEAT BUSINESS / CUMULATIVES		TOTAL ORDER VALUE FROM USERS
12			4			824
16			3			716
14			5			1016
14			1			168
17			4			1870
15			0			0
18			4			1250
18			5			1680
20			2			420
10			0			0
19			6			3160
15			6			1900
15	203	44	4	44	13,884	880
	4.6			315		
	5.5			296		
	COMPANY NORM			COMPANY NORM		

PROSPECTS

WEEK	FIRST EVER CALLS	AVERAGE CALLS ON A PROSPECT / CUMULATIVES		TOTAL CALLS ON PROS	CALLS TO PROPOSAL RATIO / CUMULATIVES		PROPOSALS SUBMITTED	PROPOSALS TO ORDER RATIO / CUMULATIVES		TOTAL ORDERS RCD FROM PROSPECTS	AVERAGE ORDER VALUE NEW BUSINESS / CUMULATIVES		TOTAL ORDER VALUE FROM PROSPECTS
14	5			6			2			1			680
15	3			8			3			2			420
16	6			11			1			3			1120
17	6			6			4			2			468
18	4			7			2			0			0
19	2			11			3			2			378
20	2			8			4			1			185
21	5			8			5			2			410
22	4			4			1			0			0
23	0			0			0			0			0
24	3			7			4			3			526
25	4			6			2			1			286
26	2	46	85	6	85	33	2	33	18	1	18	4669	196
		RATIO Z 1.8			RATIO X 2.6			RATIO Y 1.8			259		
		1.65			2.2			1.75			265		
		COMPANY NORM			COMPANY NORM			COMPANY NORM			COMPANY NORM		

SECOND QUARTER'S REPEAT BUSINESS TARGET

10,500
1st QUARTER DEFICIT

SECOND QUARTER'S NEW BUSINESS TARGET

5,750
1,205 1st QUARTER DEFICIT

SALES ANALYSIS
SECOND QUARTER   YEAR 1999   SALESPERSON J. WATSON

PRODUCT GROUP ANALYSIS

WEEK	A	B	C	D	E	F	G	H	I	J	K	L	M	N	O	P
14	1	4	5	1	0	3	2	7		2						
15	4	3	6		2		4		1							
16	1	4	7	1	1	3		8		3						
17	1	2	3		1		6		1							
18	2	2	2	1		3		8		2						
19	4	4	5	2	1	3		7		3						
20	1	3	3	1	1	2		7		2						
21	1	1	5	2		3	3	6		1						
22	2	3	4	1		2		7		1						
23		1	2			1		3								
24	3	3	6	2	2	4		6		4						
25	1	2	3	1	1	2		5		2						
26	2	1	2			1		7		1						
	22	33	52	12	6	30	38	81	46	23						

CALLS ANALYSIS

WEEK	TOTAL CALLS	BY APP'T	FROM LEAD	SERVICE CALLS
14	18	11	3	0
15	24	19	2	1
16	25	14	4	0
17	20	10	3	3
18	24	6	2	0
19	26	13	2	5
20	24	12	1	0
21	26	9	4	0
22	24	11	3	1
23	10	4	0	4
24	26	16	1	0
25	20	10	3	0
26	21	9	1	1
	288	144	29	15

CUSTOMER CATEGORY ANALYSIS

WEEK	1	2	3	4	5	6	7	8	9	10	11	12	13	14	15	16	17	18	19	20
14	6	6	1	4			1													
15	6	4	3	2	1	2	4		2	3										
16	5	3	4	2	2	3	3	1	1	1										
17	3	2	4	3	1	1	4		2											
18	4	4	2	4	2	2	4		2											
19	6	3	4	1	1	1	4	1	3	2										
20		4	3			2	3	2		2										
21	4	5	2	3	1	1	2	3	2	3										
22	3	4	3	2	2		2	3	5											
23	1	1	2		1		1		3	1										
24	7	3	2	4	1	1	2	2	4											
25	1	2	4	3			3	2	5											
26	3		2	4	2	1	3	3	2	1										
	51	41	37	33	14	14	37	17	31	13										

Apart from entering the numbers on these cards each Monday, there is no further action necessary until the end of the thirteen-week period, in our case, until after the end of week 26. Then you or your secretary total all the columns and by dividing the smaller totals into the larger for each pair of numbers on the personal performance record card (page 180), you calculate each salesperson's performance for that quarter in respect of eight different aspects of the job.

From the totals on the sales analysis master card (page 181), you pinpoint any part of the product range that J. Watson might be neglecting, and likewise for any industry important to the company. The bottom right column's totals give you information on how effective each salesperson is at making appointments, how effective your sales promotion and advertising activities have been in each territory and how much time each salesperson has been forced to spend on non-selling activities.

All the data you need, is on two A4 size cards, to pinpoint specific problems and implement remedial action without delay.

By comparing one quarter's figures with another, a pattern of personal performance can clearly be established. The ratios are also extremely valuable in calculating accurate and attainable sales targets for each salesperson, but this we have dealt with under Forecasting.

The Company Norms

If you take the quarterly totals for each of your salespeople and add them all together, you can calculate performance norms for the sales force as a whole.

The charts on the following three pages show examples of how to produce norms and sales force totals on just three pieces of specially designed card.

The value in calculating norms for performance is:

(a) Each salesperson can relate his own performance, in detail, to the average (norm) performance for the sales force as a whole.

(b) Where any salesperson has a personal performance ratio which is worse than the norm ratio, he strives during the next quarter to bring his performance at least up to the norm performance.

(c) In achieving this improvement, the company norms for the next quarter are automatically better than for the last quarter.

(d) The whole process then becomes automatic. Performance steadily improves because no one wants a ratio which is worse than the norm. You can almost sit back and let it happen.

	SALESPERSON	TOTAL CALLS	ABOR- -TIVES	CALLS ON USERS	ORDERS FROM USERS	TOTAL ORDER VALUE FROM USERS	FIRST EVER CALLS	CALLS ON PROSPTS	PROP'LS SUBM- ITTED	ORDERS FROM PROSPTS	TOTAL ORDER VALUE FROM PROSPECTS
	COMPANY NORMS					PERIOD 2ND QUARTER 1999 WEEKS 14-26					
1	J.WATSON	288	44	203	44	13,884	46	85	33	18	4,669
2	R.BRIGGS	264	32	168	27	8,963	51	96	44	27	6,463
3	L.SUTTON	249	28	202	31	9,275	36	47	11	8	2,761
4	F.WINTERS	296	31	175	27	8,740	68	121	57	31	7,892
5	G.HOPKINS	321	43	212	41	8,202	59	109	49	28	6,720
6	A.ROLFE	199	37	142	20	7,966	29	57	19	14	3,995
7	B.STEIN	255	42	170	26	8,449	56	85	39	22	5,977
8	S.ARMSTRONG	253	30	166	32	9,791	66	87	48	24	6,502
9	J.JONES	241	21	175	31	9,464	41	66	35	20	4,744
10	W.ASQUITH	302	26	204	52	13,242	64	98	52	29	8,842
11											
12											
13											
14											
15											
16											
17											
18											
19											
20											
21											
22											
23											
24											
25											
	TOTALS	2,668	334	1,817	331	97,976	516	851	387	221	58,565
		A	B	C	D	E	F	G	H	J	K

Abortive call Ratio $\frac{A\ 2668}{B\ 334}$ = 8.0 to 1

Calls to orders Ratio (Users) $\frac{C\ 1817}{D\ 331}$ = 5.5 to 1

Average order Value (Users) $\frac{E\ 97,976}{D\ 331}$ = 296

Average calls on a Prospect $\frac{G\ 851}{F\ 516}$ = 1.65

Calls to proposals Ratio (Prospects0 $\frac{G\ 851}{H\ 387}$ = 2.2 to 1

Proposals to orders Ratio (Prospects) $\frac{H\ 387}{J\ 221}$ = 1.75 to 1

Average order Value (Prospects) $\frac{K\ 58,565}{J\ 221}$ = 265

ACTIVITY ANALYSIS

PERIOD 2nd Qtr. 1992

PRODUCT GROUP TOTALS

	SALESPERSON	A	B	C	D	E	F	G	H	I	J	K	L	M	N	O	P
1	J. WATSON	22	33	52	12	6	30	38	81	46	23						
2	R. BRIGGS	26	27	57	14	41	17	32	72	46	16						
3	L. SUTTON	14	31	53	10	39	26	39	64	48	19						
4	F. WINTERS	18	29	46	13	18	18	33	53	52	24						
5	G. HOPKINS	22	24	49	11	4	17	29	66	51	29						
6	A. ROLFE	29	20	42	12	17	14	35	84	41	36						
7	B. STEIN	27	28	52	9	18	22	24	80	47	18						
8	S. ARMSTRONG	18	24	59	18	39	29	41	72	46	30						
9	J. JONES	21	20	61	14	24	26	39	77	52	24						
10	W. ASQUITH	31	23	64	12	21	32	39	69	43	37						
11																	
12																	
13																	
14																	
15																	
16																	
17																	
18																	
19																	
20																	
21																	
22																	
23																	
24																	
25																	
	TOTALS	228	259	535	125	227	241	359	723	473	235						

INDUSTRY CATEGORY TOTALS

	1	2	3	4	5	6	7	8	9	10	11	12	13	14	15	16	17	18	19	20
1	51	41	37	33	14	14	37	17	31	13										
2	52	40	35	38	11	8	19	21	31	9										
3	48	24	33	31	10	6	26	18	32	14										
4	67	31	47	34	9	9	44	11	31	22										
5	76	24	51	42	13	11	53	14	21	16										
6	32	51	17	18	4	2	14	9	40	12										
7	50	30	32	30	17	4	38	6	31	17										
8	48	33	30	36	10	4	57	17	25	12										
9	45	24	31	29	14	7	28	23	24	14										
10	71	17	53	44	22	9	42	23	13	8										
TOTALS	594	317	366	327	123	74	338	159	286	137										

	SALESPERSON	TOTAL CALLS	TOTAL BY APPOINT-MENT	% of Total	TOTAL FROM LEADS	% of Total	TOTAL SERVICE CALLS	% of Total
	ACTIVITY ANALYSIS					PERIOD 2nd Qtr. 1999		
1	J. WATSON	288	144	50	29	10	15	5.2
2	R. BRIGGS	264	192	73	26	10	17	6.4
3	L. SUTTON	249	103	41	13	5	6	2.4
4	F. WINTERS	296	244	82	18	6	14	6.4
5	G. HOPKINS	321	272	85	34	11	24	7.5
6	A. ROLFE	199	140	70	41	21	4	2.0
7	B. STEIN	255	241	95	27	11	7	2.7
8	S. ARMSTRONG	253	127	50	18	7	12	8.7
9	J. JONES	241	106	44	24	10	14	5.8
10	W. ASQUITH	302	285	94	42	14	8	2.6
11								
12								
13								
14								
15								
16								
17								
18								
19								
20								
21								
22								
23								
24								
25								
		2,668	1,854	69	272	10	136	5.1

Q

Quotations and Proposals

In the dark, satanic mills of Victorian times, men (they were always men) sat on tall stools at high desks, writing to customers with quill pens, sending them quotations. They used terminology such as: 'looking forward to receipt of your esteemed order' – 'trusting our quotation will prove to be to your satisfaction' – 'ensuring you of our best intentions' – and so on.

If your company is still using this kind of phraseology, stop it immediately. It's out of date. Take a look around. Men have got to the moon and we are in the age of instant communications.

A quotation is a prime opportunity to sell your products.

Look upon a quotation as a highly specific, one-off, direct mail shot meant not only to give specific details of your product (the specifications) but also *to sell it.*

A quotation should list as many of the benefits that the product will bring to the customer as possible.

The advantage of a quotation is that it is (or should be) based on an intimate knowledge of the product requirements and benefits the customer is looking for.

Buyers do not buy solely on price. None of us does. If we did, we'd all be running round in East European cars.

Buyers are motivated by at least two other things:

(a) Does the product or service meet their requirements (or indeed exceed them)?
(b) Is it value for money?

Cost is only part of the equation.

The quotation with the highest price may, in the estimation of the

187

buyer, be the one that provides the best value for money.

All quotations should be attractive, pleasing to the eye and easily understood – not a set of boring, standard quotation forms which have been in use since the turn of the century.

If the product is a high specification engineering tool, or a complicated financial package, the buyer will understand the technical terminology and it's fine to use it. But make it easy to read and follow in a logical way.

It is helpful to observe the following:

(a) Begin with a brief statement of the detailed objectives that you know the customer wishes to achieve through purchasing your equipment, product or service.

(b) Follow this with a brief outline or recommendations showing how your equipment, product or service will completely fulfil the customers objectives.

(c) Elaborate on item 2 with a list of additional benefits which the customer may not have thought of, which may come into play at a later stage in the product's life.

(d) With full lists of figures, explain financing, time, labour rates, maintenance costs, depreciation periods, production outputs, and whatever else is relevant, how the purchase can be justified by the buyer. All prices should include delivery, installation, commissioning or whatever else.

(e) Highlight any and all guarantees you supply. Include details of your after sales service and how it operates.

(f) Include at least three third-party references who may be contacted direct by the customer and who are prepared talk about the product in detail.

(g) Write everything in modern English and produce an attractive package. Use your company's desktop publishing facilities to produce a package that's really unique and outstanding.

(h) Add your Criteria For Ordering list.

(i)   If you've ever been asked to submit to a Supplier Evaluation Report before you get onto a customer's list of Approved Suppliers, adopt this SER as your own and include it with all quotations.

(j)   This is the big one ......

If you really want to WIN ...

... TAKE IT IN!

Don't post it. Don't fax it. Take it in personally and go through it with the customer to make sure that you have got everything right. Then close ... "Are you happy with everything then?" "Can we go ahead, then?"

R

Recruiting Salespeople

After identifying your manpower requirements, the process of recruitment starts with a recruitment advertisement. This allows you an opportunity to promote your company. So, when you enter the market looking for people, remember that you're selling, not buying.

It's all too easy to get it wrong – just take a look at the recruitment sections of the daily and Sunday broadsheets as well as those in the trade magazines.

Some advertisements are totally self-centred. They talk at length about what they want and say nothing about what's in it for the applicant. The response mechanism is a box number, which means that (a) all the best people will totally ignore the ad, (b) the second best will feel anxious in case it's their own company, whilst (c) all the useless people will apply in droves.

Other advertisements are much better – those placed by companies who know that, when they go to the trouble and expense of displaying themselves in an advertisement, they might as well have a go at selling the company (and the product) as well as finding the people they are looking for.

They will have paid a lot of money for the advertisement, so they don't waste an opportunity for promoting themselves. Which means that *right from the opening line,* they're dangling carrots in front of the prospective applicant. They give brand names prominence, motivating the candidate to want to be associated with such a reputable and high-profile brand.

They tell potential applicants just what they can expect to get from the job. They also make them feel important and sought after. And they give them the opportunity to take instant action.

Of course, many advertisements are placed by recruitment agencies who have been given the job of screening the applicants through to short-list. Even so, these still ensure that the status and importance of the company is well represented and that anyone fortunate enough to get the job will equally gain status and importance.

A Ten-Stage Checklist for Picking Winners

1. Job Specification

Do I really need to recruit? If so, how do I wish the person to operate?

2. Person Profile

Bearing in mind the task I need performed, what qualities do I require in the person to perform it?

3. The Search

How should I advertise to attract the right type of applicant? It's going to take a lot of time to do it properly. Do I do it all myself, or should I find a good recruitment consultancy to do it for me. (Note: no recruitment consultant, however good, can prove better than a 50% success rate. But, then, neither can you.)

4. Letters, Application Forms and Photographs

What can I really discover from a letter? Do I need a (quality) application form? Would a photograph help?

5. Initial Interview

How well prepared am I to interview and to sell to the applicants? Do I conduct the initial interview over the telephone or face to face? If face to face, do I have the numbers, words and psychometric tests ready to use?

6. Second Interview

Which areas in the applicant's history need further investigation and how am I going to test the second-interview applicants in these areas? Is the draft contract of employment up to date? What about company operating procedures and company car rules?

7. References

Am I sure, in each case, that I have the telephone number of the applicant's line manager and the prepared open-ended questions I wish to ask?

8. Short List

Do I need to meet the candidate's spouse/partner? If I do, can I do it over dinner and check out their home on the way?

9. Hiring and Turning-down Letters

Will my appointment letter overcome any competition (good applicants may have more than one offer) or my turndown letter leave a good image?

10. The Welcome

How can we construct the first day to give the recruit total reassurance that he/she has made the right decision?

First Interview Procedure

A first interview should last about 30 minutes and must start promptly at the appointed time.

Open the conversation by getting the candidate to tell you about him or herself; an effective way to put the candidate at ease. First impressions are vital. If the candidate does not impress you from the start on such an important occasion, then your prospects and customers are also unlikely to be impressed.

The first 15 minutes should be devoted to finding out as much about the candidate as possible and how closely he or she fits the Person Profile. With careful questioning, encourage the applicant to do about two-thirds of the talking. Avoid giving too much information about your company at this early stage, in case the applicant is a competitor or future competitor. Much more important is to discover what he or she has taken the trouble to find out about you.

If you are seeking experienced salespeople, you should expect to see 'well-done' memos, league tables, commission statements and turnover graphs – all showing evidence of steady improvement and success.

If you are recruiting someone without sales experience, you need to check with care into such things as work habits, experience and motivation. It's surprising how many people who 'wish to enter sales' have not made the least preparation – even reading a book on Selling.

Half way through the interview, you should have reached a firm conclusion on whether or not you will be inviting the candidate for a second interview.

If so, spend the second half talking about the company and the job, building interest and enthusiasm. Remember that the applicant has to want to join your organisation as much as you want him or her. Say what the next stage will be – a second interview – and fix the date and time there and then. End by asking if there are any questions about any aspect not fully covered.

If the applicant has been unsuccessful, there's no reason why you should not say so. Try to soften the blow by explaining that the job is not right for the applicant, rather than the other way round. Remember that you are doing a PR job for your company. If you detect potential for another job, you could suggest keeping the name on file in case a more suitable position should become vacant.

Throughout the meeting, you must listen carefully for significant remarks and follow them up. Equally important, look for significant omissions. If the candidate hurries over a career event which was obviously important this is a signal for further probing.

If you have any doubts about any part of the applicant's past, present or future – bring them out into the open politely but firmly, offering the candidate a fair opportunity to answer them in full.

Do not let the interview overrun and make it clear when the meeting is over.

Immediately afterwards, note down your assessment and decision. Compare the answers you got with what the candidate wrote in the initial letter or on the applications form. NEVER use these in the first interview. And no tea or coffee! You get yours during the ten minute assessment period between interviews.

How to avoid the Losers

If your business is to succeed, you have to be able to pick winners and avoid losers. I have two pet systems for picking winners, both very simple. If you are interviewing for a sales position, all the applicants will probably be clever enough to give you all the answers you want to hear from the usual run of questions.

If I am looking for experienced people, then they have to prove that all their experience is worth something. So I challenge them to prove how good they are:

> "Okay, show me the evidence of your last seven years in this business. Show me your 'well done' letters, the commission statements, the league tables, whatever you've got that proves to me you are what you say you are."

If they can't show me anything because they've forgotten it, or never collected all the evidence in the first place, then they are off my list. They are either fools or liars – I don't want to hire either. Alternatively, I say:

> "Tell me about yourself from day two of your life, the day after you popped out of your mother's womb. Just sketch over it, to give me an idea how you grew up."

It takes people off their guard.

What I'm looking for is people who like being with other people. I'm trying to identify the loners who never join in on anything, but I don't look for the captain of the school cricket team unless I want a potential sales manager.

I'm looking for 'Indians' not 'chiefs', and I'm looking for people who 'enjoy' people – a characteristic formed in the first seven years of life.

These two methods will usually throw up four applicants out of thirty or forty who can prove a track record, and who are obviously the right sort of 'people' people.

Good 'feelings' or 'hunches' about people should be kept in abeyance until the last interview. Feelings in your water that 'this person is going to fit in', can lead you to hiring someone who you will be firing three months later. But if you have been through all the preliminaries, then you can feel safer about following your instincts, particularly if you are having difficulty deciding between the last two or three people.

In the first and second interviews, you need to take all the emotion out of the job, and work to a formal system. You must work out in advance a detailed profile of the person you want, with all the specifications like age, location, marital status, financial situation, education, experience, motivation, aspirations and health all taken into consideration.

You can then draw up three grades – perfect, average and no good – for each specification. Give the interviewees marks between 0 (no good), 2 (average) or 4 (perfect) in each category. At the end of the interviews, you simply tot up the totals and the highest scores are the people who should be seen again. This is an ideal checklist for a preliminary telephone interview. A simple example is shown on the next page.

So, provided you get the profile right in advance, it should all happen hunch-free.

PERSON PROFILE FOR SELECTING A SALESPERSON

FINALISE DETAILS BEFORE DRAFTING ADVERTISEMENTS - USE FOR TELEPHONE SCREENING AND ON FIRST INTERVIEWS

APPLICANT'S NAME

ADDRESS

TELEPHONE NUMBER

SCORE

								SCORE
AGE	25 TO 33	4	FROM 22 TO 37	2	UNDER 22 OR OVER 37	0	
LOCATION	BRISTOL	4	WITHIN 5 MILES RADIUS OF BRISTOL	2	OUTSIDE 5 MILES RADIUS OF BRISTOL	0	
MARITAL STATUS	MARRIED WITH CHILDREN	4	SINGLE/MAR'D WITH NO CHILDREN	2	DIVORCED OR SEPARATED	0	
FINANCIAL SITUATION	ASSETS AND REASONABLE MORTGAGE	4	NO DEBTS AND NO MORTGAGE	2	NO ASSETS AND SOME DEBTS	0	
EDUCATION	O's OR CSEs + FURTHER TRAINING	4	CSEs WITH NO FURTHER TRAINING	2	NO QUALIFIC-ATIONS	0	
EXPERIENCE	WELL TRAINED IN SELLING	4	SOME SALES HISTORY	2	NO SALES HISTORY	0	
EXPERIENCE IN MARKETS	COMPREHEN-SIVE EXPERIENCE	4	SOME EXPERIENCE	2	NO EXPERIENCE	0	
KNOWLEDGE OF PRODUCTS	FULL KNOWLEDGE	4	SOME KNOWLEDGE	2	NO KNOWLEDGE	0	
MOTIVATION	HIGHLY FINANCIALLY MOTIVATED	4	STAUS CONSCIOUS	2	WANTS CAR AND FREEDOM	0	
ASPIRATIONS	KEEN TO DEVELOP AS SALESPERS'N	4	MOVE INTO MANAGEMENT	2	NO VIEWS HELD	0	
HEALTH	EXTREMELY FIT	4	IN GOOD HEALTH	2	UNHEALTHY AND UNFIT	0	
					TOTAL SCORE		

Questions for the Interviewee

'A candidate under stress has greater allegiance to his/her emotional safety than to the truth'. Kurt Einstein

So ...

You must have a comfortable, stress-free, pressure-free situation for an interview.

Every question must feel comfortable to you – or don't use it.

And ... the candidate's first answer to any questions will likely be the 'programmed' answer. It is the follow-up 'why?' question that gets the spontaneous, more truthful answer.

Some suggested questions

(a) *'What have you been criticised for during the last four years?'*

If the answer is 'Nothing' – don't employ. Such a response indicates inflexibility to be trained or managed. If the candidate tells you the criticisms, then ask, *'Did you agree or disagree with that criticism?'* If they totally disagreed with the criticism – don't employ. Same reasons. *'Did you agree with anything?* Check question.

(b) *'Where would you like to be in three or five years time?'*
'How do you expect to get there?'
'When will you think you have arrived?' (Success!)

Beware of candidates who say, 'I will never arrive.' Compulsive achievers – unhealthy. Short term assets – long term liabilities.

(c) *'Describe to me your ideal boss.'*
'And your least ideal boss.'

(d) *'What kind of people do you enjoy the most?'*

(e) *'Can you lie?'*

The most likely answer is 'Yes, but I'd prefer not to.' Follow up with *'When would you lie? Give me three instances.'*

(f) 'What do you enjoy most in a job? And what least?'

This pin-points strengths and weaknesses. Match the answers to your job specification, because 'enjoy' is strengths and 'least' is weaknesses. Can you train up the 'leasts'?

(g) 'How would you describe yourself – with three adjectives?'

Follow this up with, *'Why do you feel this word fits you?'* It is likely that all three adjectives will be positives. So go on to ask, *'You must have a few negatives too. Give me three.'* In turn, this can be followed with, *'What are you going to do to improve on them?'*

References

Any job offer must be 'subject to satisfactory references', and always take up references – BY TELEPHONE.

With the successful candidate's prior permission, telephone his or her past immediate line managers. Ask the right open-ended questions to get the answers you need, and to clarify any obscurities. Listen carefully to what is said. How it is said and what is omitted.

Ask for a written reference as well – for what it's worth! No ex-manager will put anything really bad in print, but your personnel department probably expects something in writing.

For experienced sales candidates, also check with a few of their current customers.

Psychometric Testing

Psychometric testing is an essential tool in the recruitment, selection and development process. All employers owe it to themselves and their workforce to use the best of all methods available to chose those all-important people who make future success possible.

But what's wrong, you may ask, with the good old application form, references and final interview? Well, absolutely nothing if you want to find out how well a person can complete application forms or handle standard interview questions.

Incorporating a range of psychometric measures into the selection process dramatically improves accuracy in recruitment. There is plenty of material in the market concerning psychometric testing. Read it and see how it may be incorporated into your recruitment process.

Reward

Job Security

The first area of reward that we are going to look at is one of the most important and also one of the cheapest methods, and it forms the foundation of motivating your sales people – job security. No-one is guaranteed a job for life, but effective sales people deserve at the very least a secure job, and sales managers need to know that tomorrow morning their sales team will be out winning new business, not sitting in the car reading the 'Appointments Pages' of the *Daily Telegraph*.

So how are we going to achieve this?

(a) **Contact** – the first way is regular contact with the boss. Too many sales staff only hear from their boss once a week – usually for a reprimand. You should phone your sales staff regularly and meet with them face to face as often as possible. It's a lonely life out there and they need the reassurance that the company cares.

(b) **Targets** – the second way to ensure job security is to set achievable sales targets. You can set your sales staff whatever targets your company requires. It can be the number of calls per day or week, the number of orders generated, the number of miles driven or the value of the orders obtained, whatever you need. But, make sure they are achievable and tailored to the potential of both the individual and the customer. There's little point setting every member of your sales team a flat 10% increase just because that's what the company overall requires. And whatever you do, don't move the goal posts!

I remember in one company being the top performer and every month for 3 months the targets were increased retrospectively to ensure that I failed like everyone else. Three months later I was working elsewhere. Don't lose your good performers. Don't set monthly targets more than three months in advance. None of you has a crystal ball. However, this doesn't mean to say you should set easy targets for poor performing salespeople. It's the sales manager's job to ensure that either you don't employ poor salespeople, or that you train them to become more effective ... which leads me onto my next point.

(c) **Training** – If I asked you to do fifty press-ups, not many of you would be able to achieve it. And no matter now much I shouted or threatened you, you would still not be able to achieve it. But – I could devise a training session which would help you get there over the next few weeks. The idea is to stretch your sales staff, not stress them. You can set your sales staff whatever target your company requires, providing you also make them competent to achieve that target and give them the necessary time to achieve it.

What better way to reassure your sales staff that they will be part of the company's future than to spend the company's time and money training them. And what short-term benefits can you expect if they're better trained sellers? You are also training tomorrow's management.

There are still companies who fire the bottom six salespeople at the end of every target period. And why do you think car dealers have such a high turnover of sales staff? Could it be because the boss of one of the principal training organisations of car dealerships believes and preaches that the entire sales force should be fired every 18 months and replaced with new blood.

That is not the way forward. The big stick may have worked well in years gone by, but it is almost totally ineffective in today's social environment. So build your sales force into being part of the team – don't let them believe that firing will continue until sales improve. Under those circumstances, sales rarely improve.

Company Car

Salespeople, especially men, are highly motivated by and very interested in their cars. Men see their car as an extension of their virility, hence the need for the car to be big and red and with electric windows. So what can you do with a car to reward your sales staff?

What about a red C Series Mercedes saloon? Imagine driving home in this and parking it on the drive one evening. How much happier would a salesperson be getting into this in the morning and going off to his or her first call rather than in a Escort 1300. If you could convert that enthusiasm into additional sales how much more profitable would your company become?

So, should you give them all a Merc? Maybe. The additional cost of running this car over your standard salesperson's car is surprisingly small, yet the benefits could be surprisingly large. Or, what about a top of the range 500SL sports? How much would this turn on your sales staff? Should you give them all a Merc sports? Probably not, but there is a way that you can give one of them a top of the range car as a reward for performance.

If you have a fair number of sales people, why not give your top performer every month the opportunity to drive around in a Merc. Sports instead of his or her Escort? You can do it for almost no extra cost. The big advantage of doing it on a monthly basis is that the winner cannot get used to the car because a month is a relatively short period of time. So, half way through the month he or she should still be motivated enough to win the car again. Yet, every other member of the sales team still has the opportunity of winning it off him or her, thus maintaining their motivation. But, you must make sure that the same person doesn't win it every month. You do this by ensuring that the targets are fair every month and adjusting them accordingly to the potential of the area as we have already discussed.

What about the colour of the company car? What a nonsense it is to insist that sales people must have a corporate colour. Of course, you should exclude the cheap and cheerful colours if you want to maintain a quality image as a company, but remember that 95% of your customers never see your vehicles. And don't forget that for your sales staff, the company car is also their office and they spend approximately one third of their time driving around in it. So get as much reward and motivation as you can out of a choice of colour – it's free!

And what about the type of car? You should make sure that whilst this is a dangerously political and emotional subject, the needs of the business and the salesperson should outweigh the internal politics. Sales staff with a large area such as Scotland are more likely to require a comfortable cruiser or 4x4 for long distances, whereas someone looking after the inner M25 area is more likely to want an automatic or a Gti which is small and nippy.

Selling is our job, so don't let the opinions and jealousies of people who have a company car as a perk have a demotivating effect on your sales people. They need the car as an essential tool to do their job. And if you can get them a car with air conditioning, go for it. Many cars have air-con built in these days free. How many of you have arrived at a customer at 10.00 in the morning with the sweat already running down your back. Wouldn't your customers prefer to see a cool and alert salesperson rather than a sweating and dishevelled one.

If you can't afford a top of the range Merc – as I can't in my small company – there is still another way of engendering motivation. Why not let your top performer borrow the Managing Director's car for a weekend? My top salesperson every month takes home my Calibra Turbo and I drive around in his or her Escort. They won't take my wife though!

One word of warning. Don't use the car as a booby prize. You've all heard stories of the worst performer having a Reliant Robin. It's not beneficial and it certainly won't motivate anybody in your company. In fact, it will have exactly the opposite effect.

Status

Next topic – status. First of all we have the organisation chart. Now we all know that this chart represents the reporting structure and not the ranking. However, your sales staff, who are at the end of a reporting leg, always appear at the very bottom of the chart – at the same level as the cleaners and warehouse staff. So, they see themselves at that level of the organisation. Why not move them half way up the page? It costs nothing and it will make them feel more important.

In the first chart overleaf you see the the structure of a typical company, with the Chief Executive believing himself to be at the top of the heap and customers somewhere down at the bottom – not necessarily part of the same story.

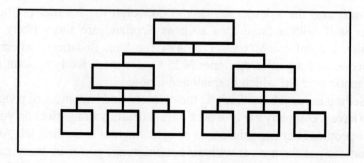

However, the latest thinking and a more relevant organisation structure is the inverted pyramid set out below, with the customers (as the most important people in the organisation) at the top and the Chief Executive supporting the whole structure from the bottom. Now you can tell your sales staff that they are the most important link between customers and company.

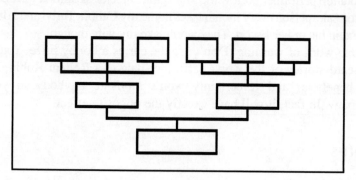

Job Titles and Business Cards

Now, why is it difficult for sales reps to get past receptionists and secretaries? Because they are called 'sales reps'. Do Managing Directors or Sales Directors ever have problems getting to speak to important decision makers? No, of course not. Why? Because their titles show that they are important people.

So, if you can improve your sales peoples' job titles to make them appear more important, they are likely to get to more decision makers.

How much more business would this win you?

What do you get if you change your sales reps' job titles.

Two things. The first – motivated staff. How many among you have had an internal promotion or taken on a new and bigger job?

When you first got your new business cards, how did you feel when you looked at your new job title – 'Sales Manager' 'Sales Director' 'Managing Director'? Did it make you feel good? Yes, of course it did, and you can make your sales people feel just as good. You could call them area sales managers, regional sales managers, business development managers, profit improvement manager or even, if you're bold enough, area sales directors or field sales directors. Of course, other people in your organisation need to know that they're not board directors and that the job title is for external use only.

The second reason is that it will help them get their foot in the door of your customers and potential customers. It will help them get more appointments with important decision makers, which can only lead to your company getting more business.

What about their business cards? If you have a sales manager of the year, why not put that on his business card, or print names in gold to make them stand out more?

So don't forget, the bigger the job title the better.

Oh, and one other benefit. It also makes it more difficult for your sales staff to be poached by your competitors.

Prizes

Small prizes are the most under-used rewards of all. They can be very inexpensive yet highly motivational. They need not be restricted to your external sales force, they can also be used productively for tele-sales, customer service and trade counter staff.

There are many simple things you can do. Things like putting a bottle of champagne or wine in full view of the middle of the office with a notice attached saying that, at the end of the week, the bottle will go to whoever has generated the most leads, most appointments, the first to hit target, the biggest conversion rate – whatever you like. Or you can pin a pair of theatre or cinema tickets to your internal notice board. The important thing is to make the prizes visible, which means your staff will see them as tangible. The costs are only about £40 to £50 per week.

At Christmas last year I wandered around the company every day with an advent calendar full of little chocolates and every day the first member of staff to be able to recite our mission statement won the chocolate.

How about giving your top performer each month a weekend in Paris? It would probably only cost £250 and if targets were set fairly and evenly, would surely cover itself by increased sales. In one of my previous jobs, where we had a number of sales people, we used to award the salesperson of the month a small silver plated cup. It wasn't big or extravagant and only cost between £10 to £15, but a small cup engraved with 'Salesperson of the Month' or 'Top Performer of the Month', forever displayed on the mantelpiece at home, was highly motivational for the winners. Keep a big cup for the full year. Once again you are only talking £30 or £40.

Another method I find very effective is for the boss to have bets with the staff like, 'I bet you can't beat your sales target by 10% this week'. I usually bet a pint of beer or a box of chocolates so it only costs a couple of pounds. But, you should make sure that your staff only wins half the time whilst you win the other half. This keeps them on their toes. Pay or present the prize publicly. There's nothing more rewarding in business than seeing the boss dip his hand into his own pocket.

These little ideas will help to make your work fun. Small prizes given out frequently ensure that a wide variety of people have the opportunity to win something. However, make sure that whatever you give is reasonable quality. You don't have to give the crown jewels, but make sure that you don't give them a Del Boy Trotter earring. At the very least, give them a pair of earrings.

SurPrizes WORK! It's highly rewarding and motivational to suddenly present a box of chocolates, a bunch of flowers or a bottle of wine to someone not expecting it, because they have performed outstandingly during that week. It's not just the value of the goods that matter – it's also the gesture.

Praise and Thanks

The only place you see the words 'WELL DONE' these days is on the menu at a steak house. Your right hand is probably the most important motivational instrument in your company. Employ a bit of MBWA. For the uninitiated, this is the art of Managing by Wandering About, the point of which is to try to catch somebody doing something right. Don't miss a single opportunity to say 'Well done' and give them a pat on the back.

What about sending a note to the salesperson's home? Such notes should be very brief – 'thank you for the big order you won last week', 'well done for beating your sales targets – good work', 'I notice you got an inquiry after weeks of long negotiations', 'thanks for the long hours put in over this project'. It's especially beneficial to have these short notes hand-written rather than typed. They then become a personal gesture which, if mailed, your salesperson's spouse or partner will also see. This allows them also to bask in the glory – some compensation for the many telephone calls and interruptions that inevitably hit a salesperson at home.

At the end of each year, at the very least, drop your salespeople a line saying thanks for the hard work. I always do this at salary review. Don't just tell somebody in the corridor that they've had a pay rise, send a letter to their home and congratulate them on their hard work. Having said that, written praise should never, ever replace face to face thanks. It should be used in addition to meetings or telephone messages. Praise and thanks will cost you nothing other than a little bit of thought and time. But they will generate enormous results.

Money

Finally, and most importantly, we move on to money. You've all been on the courses advising you that people are not motivated by money as a primary motivator. Well let me tell you, sales people more than any other group are influenced by money. The nature of their personality makes it much more likely that they want a cruise or a skiing holiday or quality branded clothes or to spend more time eating and drinking. By their very competitive nature they want to keep up with the Joneses. So how do you motivate them with money? First of all, it's important that the sales manager is aware of the financial status of each member of his team. Someone with no debt is less likely to be financially hungry than someone with an enormous mortgage.

The salary you pay should cover the basics; housing, food, day to day bills. On top of this, you can incentivise and reward people in a number of ways. First, there is the ever-popular commission. Some companies pay a basic salary and a small commission on all sales. This is not as effective as paying a larger commission on all sales over and above an agreed target. Commission should reflect personal effort, not just orders that would come in anyway, even when the salesperson isn't working. Or you can pay a bonus, based upon hitting the target every month, making it open-ended over and above target. If the bonus is self-financing, and it should be, then why cap it? Why not let the sales staff sell and earn as much as they possibly can? Bonuses should also reflect profit. Build in a provision for covering bad debt. Sales people have to be part of the recovery team as well as the sales team.

If you pay a bonus by simply putting the cash in with their pay every month, you'll be missing a big opportunity. Firstly, you will be at least one month behind the achievement of the figures. Also, after the usual deductions, the net amount can often be 'lost' or overlooked or simply not appreciated by the sales team. So why doesn't the Managing Director or the Sales Director personally pay all bonuses every month by cheque? I pay mine gross, before deductions, but make sure the staff know that the tax will be coming out of their next month's pay. Also, I pay them the week after the sales achievement. So, the result is fast allowing, the motivation to continue into the following month. Use bonuses to reward big successes. Don't give someone an enormous pay rise. What will happen next year if they don't repeat the success? Will you take it away? No, of course you can't.

Make sure also that the value of the prize or bonus that you give reflects the status and expectation of the people that you expect to win. £10 a week bonus is unlikely to motivate a £25k a year person, whereas it would probably motivate a £12k a year telesales operator, who would feel appreciated and rewarded. Cash bonuses, like prizes and surprises, are more effective if given in small doses – very frequently. There may still be a case for having a salesperson of the year competition or bonus, although you'll find that, in the early months, at least half your sales team won't feel they can win it. Which means they may not make any additional effort till maybe halfway through the year.

But, if you do decide to pay someone £2,000, in cash, as a bonus, then pay it in five pound notes. And not into their pay. Pay it very publicly. But be careful – don't make the following kind of mistakes when you present it ...

At the 1987 National Sales Convention, a very successful sales director, Dave Brown, won a 'Sales Booster of the Year' Award, for a closing and referral technique now known as the 'You're Pulling My Leg' close. Dave still remembers the day he won his first star prize – Top Salesman for the Year. In front of 500 cheering salespeople, his managing director presented him with a briefcase containing £2000 in cash. Dave felt ten feet tall. He sat down, basking in the glory, when the finance director at the table next to him leaned over and said,

'You can't spend all that you know. 40% will go in tax.'

Suddenly, he didn't feel quite so happy, but – what the hell – he still felt pretty good. Then the Managing Director made his way towards him. He felt sure that he was going to get more congratulations and yet another pat on the back. Instead, the Managing Director stopped in front of him and said

'Can I have my briefcase back?'

Suddenly, Dave felt totally gutted. All the benefits of motivation for this important reward had been lost. Then and there, he vowed that, throughout his career, he would never allow anyone to feel as badly as he felt at that moment.

S

Service Contracts

Make sure your employees can't steal your business.

Everyone in selling – the salesperson, the area manager, the sales manager, the sales director – should have a written service contract. Not just the bare minimum to satisfy the legal requirements of the Contracts of Employment Act and the Employment Protection Acts, but a meaningful document which clearly defines what is what.

A properly designed service contract can do a lot to alleviate worry – that cancer which eats away at a person's performance in times when the going gets rough, when business is hard to get, or when personalities clash. And you know it – there are plenty of those times.

A good service contract protects both employee and employer – and it should. Here is a sample contract which could be tailored to fit practically everyone in the sales team, from salespeople to directors.

An example is set out on the following pages.

CRITICALLY IMPORTANT

Introduce the Employment Contract and the Company/ Company Car Rules during the Second Recruitment Interview.

SAMPLE EMPLOYMENT CONTRACT
Drafted for John Fenton Training International PLC by
Shoosmiths & Harrison
52-54 The Green
Banbury
Oxon, OX16 9AB

THIS CONTRACT OF EMPLOYMENT is made the .... day of ....
One Thousand Nine Hundred and Ninety.................... BETWEEN
.... whose registered office is at ....
('the Company') AND .... ('the Employee)

NOW IT IS AGREED as follows:

Term of Employment
The company shall employ the Employee as its .... and
subject to the provisions of Paragraphs 14 and 15 hereof such employment
shall be determined by either giving to the other .... months' notice in
writing of such intended determination such notice to expire at or on any day
after the end of the said period.

Duties
As...the Employee shall:

a. undertake such duties and exercise such powers in relation to the
    Company and its business as the Board of Directors (hereinafter referred
    to as the Board) shall from time to time assign to or vest in him and without
    prejudice to the generality of the foregoing those duties and powers shall
    include the following:

    (i)
    (ii)
    (iii)
    (iv)
    (v)
    (vi)

b. in the discharge of such duties and in the exercise of such powers observe
    and comply with all resolutions regulations and directions from time to time
    made or given by the Board;

c. devote substantially the whole of his time and attention during business
    hours to the discharge of his duties hereunder;

d. conform to such hours of work as may from time to time be reasonably
    required of him and not be entitled to receive any remuneration for work
    performed outside his normal hours.

211

Exclusion of other Occupations

The Employee shall not without the consent of the Company during the continuance of this Agreement be engaged or interested either directly or indirectly in any capacity in any trade business or occupation whatsoever other than the business of the Company but so that this provision shall not prohibit the holding whether directly or through nominees of quoted investments so long as not more than ten per cent of the share or stock of any class of any one Company shall be so held.

Confidential Information

The Employee shall not except as authorised or required by his duties reveal to any person persons or Company any of the trade secrets or confidential operations processes or dealings or any information concerning the organisation which may come to his knowledge during his employment hereunder and shall keep with complete secrecy all confidential information entrusted to him and shall not use or attempt to use any such information in any manner which may injure or cause loss either directly or indirectly to the Company or its business or may be likely so to do. This restriction shall continue to apply after the termination of this Agreement without limit in point of time but shall cease to apply to information or knowledge which may come into public domain.

Since the Employee also may obtain in the course of his employment by reason of services rendered for or offices held in any subsidiary company of the Company knowledge of the trade secrets or other confidential information of such company the Employee hereby agrees that he will at the request and cost of the Company enter into a direct agreement or undertaking with such company whereby he will accept restrictions corresponding to the restrictions herein contained (or such of them as may be appropriate in the circumstances) in relation to such products and such area and for such period as such company may reasonably require for the protection of its legitimate interests;

Notes and Memoranda

The Employee shall not during the continuance of this Agreement make otherwise than for the benefit of the Company any notes or memoranda relating to any matter within the scope of the business of the Company or concerning any of its dealings or affairs not permit to be used any such notes or memoranda otherwise than for the benefit of the Company it being the intention of the parties hereto that all such notes or memoranda made by the Employee shall be the property of the Company and left at its registered office upon the termination of the Employee's employment hereunder.

Return of Company's Documents and Property

Immediately on the termination of his employment hereunder the Employee shall return to the Company at.......................... all papers documents and other property in his possession in connection with his said employment and shall retain no other copies thereof without the Company's permission in writing.

Restrictive Covenants

The Employee hereby covenants with the Company that (except with the prior written consent of the company) he will not:

a. for a period of one year from the date of termination of his employment hereunder be interested or concerned directly or indirectly with any business company or firm carrying on business in England which is competitive or calculated or likely to be competitive with the business of the Company;

b. for a period of one year from the date of termination of his employment hereunder directly or indirectly solicit otherwise than for the Company orders for goods or services similar to those provided by the Company during the year prior to the termination of his employment hereunder from any person firm or company who or which is at the date of the termination of the Employee's employment hereunder or has at any time within the three years prior thereto been a customer of the Company or attempt to discourage any such person firm or company from dealing with the Company.

c. for the said period of one year directly or indirectly solicit for employment any person then employed by the Company or who was so employed during the three years prior to the termination of the Employee's employment hereunder or discourage any person then employed by the Company from continuing to be so employed;

d. at any time hereafter make use of or disclose to any third party any information of a secret or confidential nature relating to any business or affairs of the Company otherwise than in the course of his duties for or services to the Company;

e. at any time after the termination of his employment hereunder in relation to any trade or business carried on within the United Kingdom use any corporate name or trade name including the words...................... and shall use all reasonable efforts to procure that no such name shall be so used by any person firm or company with which he is connected.

Each of the covenants contained in each of the previous Sub-Paragraphs of this Paragraph shall be and is a separate covenant by the Employee and shall be enforceable by the Company independently of its right to enforce any one or more of the other covenants contained in this Paragraph.

Inventions

Where the Employee makes an invention in the course of his normal duties or in the course of duties falling outside his normal duties but specifically assigned to him, and the circumstances in either case are such that an invention might reasonably be expected to result from the carrying out of his duties or an invention is made in the course of the duties of the Employee and at the time of making the invention is made in the course of the duties of the Employee and at the time of making the invention, because of the nature of his duties, he has a special obligation to further the Company's interests, such invention shall as between the Employee and the Company be taken to belong to the Company. An 'invention' shall be taken to be that specified in a claim of the specification in any application for a patent or in the patent as interpreted by the description and any drawings obtained in the specification.

Where the Employee makes or discovers any design drawing or model or devises any method of testing or any improvement in methods of production manufacture packaging description or marketing, in all cases relating to the business of the Company or to any other business which might conveniently or otherwise be carried on in conjunction with the Company's present or future business, he shall as soon as practicable reveal the same in writing to............ keeping the same confidential and if the Company notifies the Employee that it is interested in acquiring the subject matter the same shall become the property of the Company.

Where the Employee becomes possessed of any rights in any invention or other intellectual property ('subject matter') made by the Employee which is not the property of the Company under the foregoing provisions he shall inform the Company thereof and shall as soon as practicable give details thereof and of the terms upon which he is prepared to assign such rights or grant a license in the rights for such subject matter, and the Company shall have the right to first refusal to take an assignment of or a license for the rights in such subject matter. The said right of first refusal shall be exercised within a period of three months from the notification of the terms on which rights are offered. Should the Company decide not to take up rights in the said subject matter on the terms offered (whether by refusal or by counter-offer) such rights shall not be offered to any other party on more favourable terms.

Salary

Subject as hereinafter provided the Company shall pay to the Employee during the continuance of his employment hereunder a salary at the rate of £ .... per annum (or such a higher rate as may from time to time be agreed between the parties or determined upon and notified to the Employee by the Company). In the event of any increase of salary being so agreed or notified such increase shall thereafter have effect as if it were specifically provided for as a term of this Agreement. The said salary shall be payable by equal monthly installments (and proportionately for any lesser period each monthly installment being deemed to accrue rateably from day to day) in arrears on the last day of each month.

Commission

The Company shall during the continuance of this Agreement pay to the Employee a commission of........................

Motor Car

The Company shall provide and maintain for the sole use of the Employee while on the business of the Company a motor car of suitable type on the terms set out in the Company's written rules for the use of Company cars which are set out in the Schedule hereto. On the termination of this Agreement from whatever cause arising the Employee shall immediately return the motor car to the Company at... and shall be responsible for any damage to or fault not attributable to fair wear and tear.

Expenses

The Employee shall be reimbursed all travelling hotel and other out-of-pocket expenses reasonably incurred by him in or about the discharge of his duties hereunder subject to the submission by the Employee to the Company of an expenses claim in proper form with written receipts attached. Such reimbursement will be made by the Company monthly in arrears on receipt from the Employee of his said expenses claim for that month.

Holidays

The Employee shall be entitled to .... weeks holiday (exclusive of statutory and bank holidays in each year to be taken at such time as the Board shall consider most convenient having regard to the requirements of the Company's business.

Incapacity: Company's right to terminate Agreement

If the Employee shall at any time be incapacitated or prevented by illness injury accident or any other circumstance beyond his control (such incapacity or prevention being hereinafter referred to as 'the incapacity') from discharging in full his duties hereunder for a total of ninety or more days in any twelve consecutive calendar months the Company may by notice in writing to the Employee given at any time so long as the incapacity shall continue:

a. forthwith discontinue payment in whole or any part of the said salary and commission on and from such date as may be specified in the notice until the incapacity shall cease; or

b. (whether or not payment shall already have been discontinued as aforesaid) determine this Agreement forthwith or on such date as may be specified in the notice. Subject as hereinafter provided the said salary and commission shall notwithstanding the Employee's incapacity continue to be paid to the Employee in accordance with Clauses 9 and 10 in respect of the period of incapacity prior to such discontinuance or determination.

Except as expressly provided by this Clause the Employee shall not be entitled to any salary or commission in respect of any period during which he shall fail or be unable from any cause to perform all or any of his duties hereunder without prejudice to any right of action accruing or accrued to either party in respect of any breach of this Agreement.

Summary Termination by Company in certain events

This Agreement may be terminated forthwith by the Company without prior notice if the Employee shall at any time:

a. commit any serious or persistent breach of any of the provisions herein contained;

b. be guilty of any grave misconduct or wilful neglect in the discharge of his duties hereunder;

c. become bankrupt or make any arrangement or composition with his creditors;

d. become of unsound mind or if while he is a patient within the meaning of the Mental Health Act 1959 an Order shall be made in respect of his property under Section 102 of that Act or any statutory modification or re-enactment thereof;

e. be convicted of any criminal offence other than an offence which in the reasonable opinion of the Board does not affect his position as a .... of the Company;

f. become permanently incapacitated by accident or ill-health from performing his duties under this Agreement and for the purposes of this Sub-Clause incapacity for six consecutive months or for an aggregate period of nine months in any period of twelve months shall be deemed to be permanent incapacity.

If the Employee is also to be a Director of the Company

Upon the termination of this Agreement for whatsoever reason the Employee shall upon the request of the Company resign without claim for compensation from office as a Director and from all offices held by him in subsidiary companies of the Company and in the event of his failure to do so the Company is hereby irrevocably authorised to appoint some person in his name and on his behalf to execute any documents and to do all things requisite to give effect thereto.

Disputes

If at any time there is any misunderstanding or dispute arising from the Employee's employment hereunder the Employee shall report first to..............

The Employee will have a right of appeal to the Board.

Service of Notices

Notices may be given by letter or fax message addressed to the Company at its registered office for the time being and the Employee at his last known address and any such notice given by letter shall be deemed to have been given at the time at which the letter would be delivered in the ordinary course of post.

Effect of termination

The expiration or determination of this Agreement howsoever arising shall not affect such of the provisions hereof as are expressed to operate or have effect thereafter and shall be without prejudice to any right of action already accrued to either party in respect of any breach of this Agreement by the other party.

English Law

This Agreement shall be governed by the Laws of England.

This Agreement is in substitution for all previous Contracts of Service between the Company and the Employee which shall be deemed to have been terminated by mutual consent as from the date on which the Agreement commences.

AS WITNESS the hands of the parties hereto:

Skills Needs

All sales people require both education and training – education about the company and its products and training in how to sell them.

There's a big difference between education and training. Perhaps at school you got lessons in sex education – but I'm willing to bet you didn't get any training in sex (well, not in the classroom anyway).

You see the difference! Education is the what. Training is the how.

You'll want your sales people to know everything there is to know about the company and its products and you will ensure that they get it; that they are kept up to date via sales meetings, news letters and product information from the company.

Sales skills training is your responsibility.

Always bear in mind that you are rarely in a position to teach anyone anything – what you can do is create the conditions in which they learn.

Sales skills training will be conducted in the classroom and also in the field. You should devise an on-going training programme covering a sales period of at least six months which will incorporate both formal training courses, classroom role-play and syndicate sessions and on the job training.

The main areas of training are:

(a) Prospecting
(b) Pre-approach
(c) Approach
(d) The presentation
(e) Demonstrations and use of visual aids
(f) Dealing with objections
(g) Closing
(h Analysing customer potential

(i)   After sales service
(j)   Territory planning and management
(k) Completing company forms and reports
(l)   Letter and report writing
(m) Customer knowledge
(n) Personal – appearance, attitude, car and so on

Each of these training areas requires set objectives – which is to say you must be able to identify the current level of the salesperson's performance before assessing the quantifiable improvements you wish the salesperson to achieve by the end of the next sales period.

All training takes a lot of preparation and it is based upon the three Ts:

Teaching: imparting information to trainees in a way they can understand it, presenting and illustrating the material and demonstrating it in the classroom or in the field.

Trying: where the trainees try practicing the new skills themselves, perhaps in role-playing under your supervision.

Testing: ultimately, of course, the acid test comes when the trainees are on their own in the field and you see the results of the training in their increased orders.

The best method of classroom teaching is in syndicates of between four and (at most) six. Individuals who may be reluctant to contribute much in larger groups are usually prepared to open up more readily in small groups.

It is absolutely essential that you devise an on-going Personal Skills Record Form, a completed copy of which should be retained by the sales person, the other by you in their file. This should be linked to an agreed schedule of Performance Standards. An example of a Personal Skills Record Form, and related Performance Standards charts, are set out on the following pages.

ON-GOING PERSONAL SKILLS RECORD

By using the Performance Standards as a guide, rate performance under the following headings:

A = Above Standard   B = Standard   C = Needs Improvement

	date													
1 PLANNING PREPARATION														
a Information														
b Sales Tools														
c Action plan														
2 APPROACH														
a Opening remarks														
b Sales Aids														
3 PRESENTATION														
a Product knowledge														
b Selling points														
c Buyer benefits														
d Buying motives														
e Sales aids														
f Handling objections														
g Selling sequence														
h Rental														
4 CLOSING THE SALE														
a Buying signals														
b Method of close														
c Departure drill														
5 CALL ANALYSIS														
a Records. Reports, corresp.														
b Information														
c Self analysis														
6 TERRITORY MANAGEMENT														
a Use of selling time														
b Competitors' activities														
c Territory development														
7 PERSONAL														
a Appearance														
b Attitude														
Appraiser's signature														

SELLING SKILLS

	ABOVE STANDARD	STANDARD	NEEDS IMPROVEMENT
1. Planning Prep			
a) Information	Has all the relevant information for every call	Has most of the relevant information for every call	Has some relevant information for most calls
b) Sales Tools	Always carries all relevant equipment, stationery etc	Invariably carries some relevant equipment, stationery etc	Often carries some relevant equipment, stationery etc
c) Action Plan	Always prepares a detailed action plan	Invariably prepares an action plan	Often prepares an action plan
2. Approach			
a) Opening remarks	Always gains attention - skillful opening phrases and 'carrots'	Occasionally fails to gain attention - by not using 'carrots'	Seldom uses 'carrots' or skillful opening phrases
b) Sales Aids	Always uses a sales aid where appropriate	Often uses a sales aid in approach	Seldom uses a sales aid in approach
3. Presentation			
a) Product knowledge	Fully conversant with all products and applications	Well informed about all products and applications	Has some knowledge of most products and applications
b) Selling points	Knows and uses all selling points for all products	Knows most selling points for all products	Knows some selling points for most products
c) Buyer benefits	Always translates selling points into benefits	Occasionally fails to translate selling points into benefits	Sometimes translates selling points into benefits
d) Buying motives	Always makes presentation appeal to buyer's motives	Occasionally fails to make pres'n appeal to buyer's motives	Often fails to make presentation appeal to buyer's motives
e) Sales aids	Always uses them to maximum advantage	Always uses them, often to maximum advantage	Sometimes uses sales aids to advantage
f) Handling objections	Always handles objections successfully, leaving buyer satis.	Handles most objections successfully, leaving buyer satis.	Handles most obj. successfully - not always leave buyer satisfied
g) Selling sequence	Always uses correct sequence	Often uses correct sequence	Seldom uses correct sequence
4. Closing the sale			
a) Buying signals	Always recognises and acts upon buying signals	Occasionally fails to recognise and act upon buying signals	Often fails to recognise and act upon buying signals
b) Method of close	Always uses the most appropriate style of close	Occasionally fails to use the appropriate style of close	Often fails to use the appropriate style of close
c) Departure drill	Always thanks, reassures or questions buyer as appropriate	Occasionally fails to thank, reassure or question buyer	Often fails to thank, reassure or question buyer as appropriate

ADMINISTRATION SKILLS

	ABOVE STANDARD	STANDARD	NEEDS IMPROVEMENT
5. Call Analysis			
a) Records, reports correspondence	Always completed accurately, promptly and up to date	Occasionally fails to complete accurately, promptly, up to date	Always completed - not always accurate, prompt, up to date
b) Information	Always records information for future use	Occasionally fails to record information for future use	Sometimes records information for future use
c) Self Analysis	Invariably analyses personal performance	Often analyses personal performance	Seldom analyses personal performance
6. Territory Management			
a) Use of selling time	Always gains attention - skillful opening phrases and 'carrots'	Occasionally fails to gain attention - by not using 'carrots'	Seldom uses 'carrots' or skillful opening phrases
b) Competitors' activities	Always uses a sales aid where appropriate	Often uses a sales aid in approach	Seldom uses a sales aid in approach
c) Territory development	Constantly active - opening new a/cs, developing existing a/cs	Developing existing a/cs and occasionally opening new a/cs	Concentrates on existing business, seldom tries to gain new
7. Personal			
a) Appearance	Always exceptionally well turned out - a credit to the company	Always well turned out and a credit to the company	Not always well turned out and a credit to the company
b) Attitude	Always expresses a positive attitude towards the company, its products, policies and its customers	Occasionally fails to express a positive attitude to the company, its products, policies and its customers	Often expresses a negative attitude towards the company, its products, policies and customers
8. Other relevant points			

Standards

Excellence

This is the only standard you should go for. Nothing else will do. By looking for excellence in yourself and everything you do, you'll attract around you excellent people. You will select excellent sales staff who will be capable of achieving excellent results.

In everything you do – your vision, leadership, motivation, standards of performance, communication – look for achieving excellence.

An excellent sales culture is one that is entirely customer led. Your sales team will really enjoy working for you. They will not want to let you down.

Why do people need Standards?

Because, without them, their manager will never be able to say to them...

'WELL DONE!'

T

Targets

Targets are normally set, not only as totals, but also by product. Products have differing profit margins, so make sure salespeople understand that getting the total sales target is not enough Getting the target profit margin contributions is even more important.

Sales Targets

Sales targets should have three elements –

> **TOTAL**
> **RATE**
> **MIX**

All three are critical to cash flow and to profit. (See example on following page.) Rate simply means achieving the total, with the right MIX, at the right, steady, month-by-month RATE.

A samples Targets Chart is set out opposite showing a comparison of actuals and targets for each of the three elements.

	TARGET SALES	PROFIT MARGIN	FORECAST GM
PRODUCT A	£100,000	40%	£40,000
PRODUCT B	£200,000	30%	£60,000
PRODUCT C	£200,000	20%	£40,000
	£500,000		**£140,000**

	ACTUAL SALES	PROFIT MARGIN	ACTUAL G M
PRODUCT A	£30,000	40%	£12,000
PRODUCT B	£50,000	30%	£15,000
PRODUCT C	£420,000	20%	£84,000
	£500,000		**£111,000**

Made Total	Made Rate	Got Mix Wrong

RESULT: Gross Profit DOWN by £29,000 (21% below target)

Sample Targets Chart

Tele-Selling

A sales force is a very expensive animal and, on the Pareto Principle that 80% of your repeat business will be coming from 20% of your customers, all sales management worthy of the name will be looking at ways of reducing costs whilst improving effectiveness.

A number of areas in the sales operation lend themselves to using the telephone as the primary sales tool:

(a) low potential accounts
(b) making initial contacts with new outlets
(c) small repeat orders
(d) replenishing stocks with existing accounts
(e) providing emergency cover
(f) maintaining contact when salespeople are away/ on holiday
(g) new product blitzes

Teleselling, or as it is more commonly called now, *telemarketing*, has proved itself to be highly cost-effective in these and in even higher potential sales operations.

Time was, a few years back, when telesales was solely used to sell newspaper advertising and repeat orders for frozen foods. The telesales department was manned by dolly-birds in short skirts and looked upon by sales people (mainly men) as a (very) secondary adjunct to the field sales operation.

Not any more.

These days, almost anything can be sold by telephone – banking and financial products, insurance, home improvements, fmcg – even highly specified industrial products.

Telemarketing operations are now staffed by highly professional men and women and some sales managers have spent all their life in telesales, carving out for themselves good, lucrative careers.

If you don't know anything about telesales – learn.

Work out the costs. Can a telephone sales operation save you money and produce new/increased business? If you decide a telephone sales operation will be a benefit, talk to the experts. There are a number of consultants in the field. It's a professional operation and must be treated as such. Modern telephone technology has to be seen to be believed and with computerisation, orders can be taken over the telephone, processed and out of the door within minutes.

Many telephone sales presentations (often scripted) are highly professional. They secure large orders. It has been calculated that the all-in cost of a telesales call is one sixth of the all-in cost of a face to face call by a field salesperson. A telesales person can make 100 calls a day – the field sales person about 15.

If you have a telephone sales operation, or if your have salespeople or others who spend a lot of time on the phone calling from a busy sales office, get them headsets and insist they wear them. A person using a headset is 43% more productive than someone using a handheld telephone. A full, two-piece headset is the only way to achieve concentration in a busy sales office.

Telephone technique

Whether you have a telephone sales operation or not, make sure all your salespeople (including yourself) receive adequate training in telephone technique.

Many salespeople rely on their physical presence to secure sales and/or overcome basic personal deficiencies. Not so with the phone. Over the telephone, there is no physical presence to mask or overshadow a harsh voice, poor speech or an overbearing manner. Many of us are shaken rigid when we first hear ourselves on the phone.

Even if your company doesn't sell over the phone, an enormous amount of attendant and related business is conducted via the phone. Telephone techniques can affect customer relations and ultimately, sales.

Learn to improve your voice and your telephone manner. In the days when telephones had dials, there was an expression 'smile when you dial – grin when you spin'. The thinking behind this was that if you put a smile on your face (even when you didn't feel like it) your voice would express a greater degree of warmth and sincerity.

Diction, speech patterns and tone of voice can all be improved. Work on improving your telephone technique.

Territories

Good salespeople will treat their territory as their own – their province, their fiefdom – a prize possession. Nothing, but absolutely nothing happens on their territory that they don't know about – their customers, their competitors, product use, everything.

And that's the way you want your salespeople to be about their territories.

Once they've been allocated, never, never change territories unless you lose a salesperson. Then you should review the territories and boundaries BEFORE recruiting a replacement.

Targets are irretrievably linked to territory. Although the commission scheme may remain the same, it's obvious that a salesperson in London has a completely different target to the guy or girl working in the north of Scotland. Territory development is what you will be looking for from all your people and targets should reflect realistically what the territory can produce.

Testimonials

Customer Expectations

Customer expectations keep increasing remorselessly, in spite of recessions and in spite of whatever you do, or have done, to improve quality and service.

*Never, **never** take a customer for granted.*

McGraw Hill conducted a major survey not so long ago to establish the reasons why customers changed suppliers. They discovered that 60% of customers who changed suppliers, did so not because of price, nor because of any failure or reduction in quality, but because they felt they were being taken for granted.

Do not assume that a customer will know about your products or services, about your company, or about the people you do business with. You need to tell them. You need to remind them regularly.

Another keypoint – the best selling word in Selling has always been NEW. The second best selling word in Selling has always been SOLD.

But in a lot of industries, like IT, these top two words are now reversed. SOLD is now the best selling word. Customers no longer want to be innovators, at the leading edge of technology, guinea pigs. Customers today want to know who else has bought the product or service and how well and how reliably it is performing.

Client lists and Testimonial Letters are the gold bricks of the nineties.

Testimonials

How may good, useable letters from customers are buried in the files, forgotten and never to be seen again?

Dig them out. Send copies (at least 10 of each) to every salesperson. Provide display albums so that they can use the letters professionally. Add at least three customer letters to every Proposal.

How many good, useable letters from customers are there in your salespeople's files, jealously guarded, for their eyes only! Who the hell do they think they are in competition with – their own colleagues? Their own company? Get hold of those letters and circulate them to every salesperson.

A testimonial letter doesn't have to be written directly to the person using it. Any letter to any person in the company that says 'We are very pleased with what you have done for us' is effective proof anywhere and the most powerful closing tool you can get.

Targets

Set each salesperson a target and make things happen. Each salesperson must secure one new testimonial letter every month. No excuses.

After six months you will have enough letters to build them into a special brochure – 'What Our Customers Say' – about your business. Produce a new brochure with a new set of letters every six months – and eclipse your competitors.

Getting Testimonials

Your Managing Director is the best person to procure maximum response. A sample letter from the MD is set out overleaf. An 80% response rate is not unusual. Not all the replies will be good but you need to know about the bad news as well. (You must include a SAE if you expect a good return).

Sample letter requesting customer feedback

Dear Mr ...

Your company has been a valued customer for some time now. I wonder if you would be kind enough to drop me a line to tell me what you think of us as a supplier?

Are we living up to your expectations?

Are we doing everything you expected us to do?

Is there anything we are not doing that you would like us to do?

Could we be doing more for you?

It is feedback like this from our customers that enables my team and me to make sure we are steering the ship in the right direction.

You response would be extremely valuable.

Thanks in anticipation.

Yours sincerely

Richard Tennant
Managing Director

Note: Do not send these letters to the managing directors of your customer companies. They go to the contacts whom your salespeople deal with.

U

Unwinding

How do you unwind after a hard day in the office, or out in the field?

Stereo? Scotch? Squash? Sex?

You need something. I've got a Noble & Cooley drum kit permanently set up in my study with three hundred watts of stereo to back it up. Ten minutes of beating hell out of that to Elton John and I'm a new man.

People who cannot unwind get very tired very fast. Find a way that fits you, and find it fast.

Utilising Time

Time is our most precious commodity. We can always beg or borrow (stealing is not recommended) more money – but never more time. When time is linked to money, it becomes even more precious.

How salespeople spend their time has been surveyed recently as follows:

Activity	Time
Face to face selling	10%
Customer contact on the telephone	21%
Travelling and waiting	35%
Preparing quotations	17%
Administration	16%
Service work	1%
	100%

Interesting Fact: Travelling and waiting was 35% in 1971, also. But face to face selling was 40%.

The average Cost of a Field Salesperson is £55,225 per year, inclusive of all overheads and expenses

Everything that can be done to increase the time your salespeople spend talking to customers must be done. Travelling time must be reduced wherever possible.

Help your sales people plan the maximum effective number of calls in the minimum of miles travelled every day. You can do this by purchasing a large scale map of the salesperson's territory and placing map pins (different colours representing different types and importance of accounts) in the locations of customers.

A large, different coloured pin, shows where the salesperson lives.

Plan journey trips for each day of the week with the salesperson using thin thread or sight-lines... thus helping them to reduce their travelling time and increase sales time.

NEVER use major roads as territory boundaries. Use the wide open spaces where the customers pins will never be placed

Personal Time

Every evening, before close of business, decide your priorities for the following day. Jobs should fall into 'musts', 'shoulds' and 'coulds'.

Concentrate as much as possible of your time on those jobs which are important and urgent. This reduces the amount of time you have to spend on the urgent jobs which are trivial. In fact, many of us spend a great deal of our time on jobs that may be urgent but are not, in fact, important.

Thinking ahead will help you focus your time and energy on the important tasks and objectives – those that get you closer to making money.

Manager's time planning exercise

Decide how many hours you spend on work in an average week. Include travelling time: ie the hours travelling to and from home.

In the spaces 1 to 10 on the chart overleaf, list categories of tasks/activities which you expect to have to carry out in your next full working week.

In the 'hours' column, estimate how many hours you will be spending on each activity. To keep it simple – take it to the nearest half hour.

In the 'M/S/C' column, prioritise the tasks as 'Must' 'Should' or 'Could'.

In the 'A/R' column, indicate whether the tasks are 'Active' or 'Reactive'.

Now imagine that you are told – quite unexpectedly – before the week begins, that you have to attend a conference on the Thursday and Friday. You have no choice in this. Now, only 60% of your week is available. Something has to go. What will it be?

In the 'revised hours' column, write how long you will now spend on each task.

Many managers make the mistake of wanting to complete the whole task in one sitting. This is perfectionism. Perfectionism, like procrastination, is a waste of time.

Try to understand that you can't do everything at once but you can always do 'something'. So get on with parts of the job. Many tasks look daunting. So break them down. A march of a thousand miles starts with one step... and continues with single steps.

ACTIVITY	Hours in week	M/S/C	A/R	Revised hours
1				
2				
3				
4				
5				
6				
7				
8				
9				
10				
Miscellaneous				
Total activities				

Even the busiest manager can spend fifteen minutes a day for a task. Fifteen minutes a day is ninety minutes a week, or seventy-eight hours a year. Start with fifteen minutes a day and you can work up to the amount of time the task is going to take.

One step at a time will get you there.

Allow yourself thinking time ... a period every day when you have peace, free from interruptions.

The best way of ensuring you're not disturbed in your office is to have traffic lights outside the office door. Yes, traffic lights. A system of little electronic lights which show red for when, *under no circumstances*, are you to be disturbed and green for when you are available and people can come in and see you. It's the most effective system I know of for preventing people interrupting you. Maybe it's because we're all road users and we've been conditioned. Whatever, it's a far better system than secretaries, or little signs attached to the door which say 'VACANT' and 'ENGAGED' like a lavatory. (I know what 'ENGAGED' means, but I'm not sure about 'VACANT'!)

Be prepared to let some things go undealt with. Accept the fact that they may go wrong. If they're unimportant, it's not going to matter. Better to get the big things right whilst having a few minor items screw up.

Finally, don't forget to delegate. Both up and down.

Watch out for things that land on your desk from 'upstairs' through inertia. If they don't apply to you, and you can make no contribution, send them back – politely.

And make sure your sales force, secretary, admin staff and any others reporting to you are not delegating up to you jobs they should be doing.

Your job is to manage these people, not to do their jobs for them.

V

Visual Aids

People remember:

7%	**of what they hear**
23%	**of what they see**
73%	**of what they see and hear together**

Visual aids are a must – if your salespeople aren't carrying visual aids, why are they selling face to-face? Why not have the whole selling operation undertaken on the phone?

It is said that the best visual aid is the product itself. This is only partially true. The best visual aid is the product in action – the best visual aid demonstrates the benefits of the product. Advertisements for soap powder don't focus on the powder itself. They demonstrate the power of the powder – what it can achieve – and of course, a pack shot for product identification.

Many customers have video recorders and TVs in their offices. Video presentations of the product are highly effective. Similarly, still and moving pictures on salespeople's laptop screens, along with charts, diagrams, graphs etc, help bring life to the product and back up the selling message.

Leaflets and promotional material are also important, but make sure they tie in with any advertising campaign you're running or with your direct mail shots. All your visual material should have a 'house style'.

W

Weekly Meetings

Try to have meetings with your salespeople – a few at a time, perhaps those with adjacent territories – on a regular, weekly basis.

Such meetings should not be formal or 'heavy'. Have them over a drink or a cup of coffee. You can have an agenda for things to discuss but keep it relaxed, informal and friendly. By doing this you take the 'temperature' of the sales force and get a lot of informal (which means accurate and truthful) feedback that you will never receive at more formal monthly, annual and semi-annual sales meetings.

Windows of Opportunity

Often, the solution to many of our problems lies right under our nose. It's no different in selling. Although finding new customers is important, the fastest way to increased profitability is to sell more to our existing customers

It costs seven times as much to find and sell to a NEW customer as it does to sell MORE to an existing customer. So it's vital to create windows of opportunity to sell more to the existing customer base.

Here's how.

Create a 'Windows of Opportunity' form similar to the one on the next page. Across the top specify the product range your salespeople are selling. Down the side, the salespeople should write (using as many forms as they need) the names of their customers. Next, they fill in the squares where individual customers are buying specific products. The blank squares are their windows of opportunity.

Simple.

And this is the only way that identifying the windows of opportunity can work. It is also a powerful sales aid, especially when your salespeople show the forms to their customers.

WINDOWS OF OPPORTUNITY

It costs 7 times as much to find and sell to a new customer as it does
to sell MORE to an existing customer

PRODUCTS ⇒										
⇓ CUSTOMERS										

X

Xmas Presents

The only kind of Christmas present worth giving a customer is one that will stay in his or her place of business for a long time (at least until next Christmas), reminding him or her every day that you are one of the most reliable and loyal suppliers.

Cases of whisky, once drunk, are soon forgotten. Presents that the customer takes home to his or her partner are likewise out of sight and out of mind.

So don't ever lose sight of the fact that Christmas presents are part of your sales promotion budget. Give presents that are strictly sales promotion, and you maximise the return on the investment as well as avoiding all smells of bribery and corruption.

The list of things you can give customers at Christmas time is endless. Prices, too, can range from a few pence to a few hundred pounds. Whatever you choose, always make sure your company name, address and telephone number is on the gift and always bear in mind that the gift must reflect the corporate identity of your company.

What I mean by that is – if you sell cheap and cheerful products, you can bestow a cheap and cheerful gift. If you sell the best and most expensive products, your gifts need to match this.

A word on girlie calendars. Apart from being a highly competitive field, the world has moved on and not all your customers may care to display such calendars in their offices.

The perfect business gift, the ultimate, used to sit on my office desk, black and slightly sinister, bearing the name, address and telephone number of the firm that gave it to me.

A slot in its top took a 10p piece. The coin rested in the slot, making an electrical contact which caused the whole box to vibrate, heave about and emit a gravelly, graveyard-style grinding noise. A trapdoor in the top then slowly opened, a horrible green slimy hand crept out, gently took hold of the 10p coin and then – faster than the eye could follow – hand and coin were gone, trapdoor was closed tight and the black box was still and silent.

You had to witness it to appreciate the artistry of the mechanism.

So consider the factors that made this black box the ultimate business gift. It sits on your customer's desk, making him money. Every time someone tries it, he makes 10p. Your competitor visits him, sees your name on the box and says, 'What's all this then?' Customer smiles and replies, 'Cost you 10p to find out.' (Have you ever taken money off the competition before?)

If the box goes wrong, the customer loses his income from it, and the pleasure he gets from showing people the thing. So he telephones you.

Certainly you can replace it. And oh, by the way, what's happening with that job we quoted for last month?

Y

Yahoo

If you don't know what it means, look it up in the dictionary. You will be well on your way to being one when your staff start hanging notices like this all round the office:

WE THE UNWILLING,
LED BY THE UNKNOWN
ARE ACHIEVING
THE IMPOSSIBLE
FOR THE UNGRATEFUL.
WE HAVE DONE SO MUCH
FOR SO LONG
WITH SO LITTLE
THAT WE ARE NOW
QUALIFIED
TO DO ANYTHING
WITH NOTHING.

Your Personal Development Plan

Have you asked yourself the same question you ask your job applicants... where do you want to be in five years time?

And have you answered it?

Have you identified how much you will be earning, what position in the company you will be filling, which company you want to be working for.

If you haven't, then you don't have much of a personal development plan.

Take time to closely identify your strengths and weaknesses. Work out what training you are going to require over the next few years.

In a good company, you should be allowed at least ten internal or outside course training days a year; with every two years or so, a two- or three-week residential training course.

Try and keep a journal, not necessarily daily, but of events.

Record your successes and what you think led up to them. Equally, recall your failures. Not the minor irritating ones, but the things that really went badly wrong. Identify why, so that next time in the same situation, you have something written down that can help you avoid the errors. You can learn both from your mistakes and your successes.

And get cracking with training up your successor – otherwise YOU will never get promoted.

The Indispensable Man

Sometime, when you're feeling important,
Sometime, when your ego's in bloom,
Sometime, when you take it for granted,
You're the best informed man in the room.

Take a bucket and fill it with water,
Put your hand in it up to the wrist,
Pull it out and the hole that remains there
Is the measure of how you'll be missed.

You may splash all you please as you enter,
You may stir up the water galore
But stop! And you'll see in a moment
That it looks just the same as before.

The moral of this simple story
Is do just the best that you can,
'Cause you'll find that in spite of vainglory
There's no 'indispensable man'.

Z

Zest

Don't ever let the zest go out of the job. Don't let the top brass get you down or the job start running you. If you do, you might as well give up and start growing mushrooms.

Your job satisfaction is just as important as your salespeople's.

Always let your salespeople see your best side. Keep that Wet-Thursday-in-Workington feeling for when you get home. I know it's not fair on your spouse or partner, but they'll understand (so long as it doesn't happen too often). Your salespeople won't.

Don't sabotage yourself

Don't smoke. Limit your alcohol intake. Eat well and properly – which means avoiding junk food. Take up some sport or activity which gets your mind off the job for a few hours. Whilst you are playing or working at the activity, your subconscious will still be working. This is fine – it's your subconscious which produces your most creative ideas.

Lead a balanced life

And above all ... **retain your zest**.

I hope this book will help you put a little more zest into the job and your life and provide you with a few tips which can help increase your job satisfaction, your results and your take-home pay.